Pocket
STOCKHOLM
TOP SIGHTS • LOCAL LIFE • MADE EASY

Charles Rawlings-Way, Becky Ohlsen

In This Book

QuickStart Guide

Your keys to understanding the city – we help you decide what to do and how to do it

Need to Know
Tips for a smooth trip

Neighbourhoods
What's where

Explore Stockholm

The best things to see and do, neighbourhood by neighbourhood

Top Sights
Make the most of your visit

Local Life
The insider's city

The Best of Stockholm

The city's highlights in handy lists to help you plan

Best Walks
See the city on foot

Stockholm's Best...
The best experiences

Survival Guide

Tips and tricks for a seamless, hassle-free city experience

Getting Around
Travel like a local

Essential Information
Including where to stay

Our selection of the city's best places to eat, drink and experience:

◉ **Sights**

✖ **Eating**

🅿 **Drinking**

★ **Entertainment**

🅰 **Shopping**

These symbols give you the vital information for each listing:

♪ Telephone Numbers	👪 Family-Friendly
✆ Opening Hours	🐾 Pet-Friendly
🅿 Parking	🚌 Bus
❖ Nonsmoking	⛴ Ferry
@ Internet Access	Ⓜ Metro
📶 Wi-Fi Access	Ⓢ Subway
✈ Vegetarian Selection	🚋 Tram
📖 English-Language Menu	🚆 Train

Find each listing quickly on maps for each neighbourhood:

Bar Hemingway

16 🅿 Map p233, B2

Legend has it that Hemi
self, wielding a machine
rate this timber-pan
ered bar during
showpiece is a
en by Papa ar
town. Dress
s.com; Hôtel Rit
; ✆6.30pm-2a

6 ◉ Plac

Lonely Planet's Stockholm

Lonely Planet Pocket Guides are designed to get you straight to the heart of the city.

Inside you'll find all the must-see sights, plus tips to make your visit to each one really memorable. We've split the city into easy-to-navigate neighbourhoods and provided clear maps so you'll find your way around with ease. Our expert authors have searched out the best of the city: walks, food, nightlife and shopping, to name a few. Because you want to explore, our 'Local Life' pages will take you to some of the most exciting areas to experience the real Stockholm.

And of course you'll find all the practical tips you need for a smooth trip: itineraries for short visits, how to get around, and how much to tip the guy who serves you a drink at the end of a long day's exploration.

It's your guarantee of a really great experience.

Our Promise

You can trust our travel information because Lonely Planet authors visit the places we write about, each and every edition. We never accept freebies for positive coverage, so you can rely on us to tell it like it is.

The Best of Stockholm 125

Stockholm's Best Walks

Stockholm's Best ...

Survival Guide 145

QuickStart Guide

Welcome to Stockholm

Stockholmers call their compact, walkable city 'Beauty on Water'. But despite the gorgeous old town centre Gamla Stan, Stockholm is no museum piece: it's modern, dynamic and ever-changing. This is a city of food obsessives, with good design a given across all aspects of daily life: if something can be beautiful as well as functional, why not make it so?

Gamla Stan (p22)
LEOKS/SHUTTERSTOCK ©

Stockholm
Top Sights

Skansen (p52)

Excellent outdoor
Swedish history museum.

Vasamuseet (p56)

Study the 1628 shipwreck
Vasa.

Kungliga Slottet (p24)

The world's grandest royal palace.

Millesgården (p94)

Sculptor Carl Milles' wonderful estate.

Stadshuset (p100)

Guided tours of the City Hall.

Historiska Museet (p84)

10,000 years of Swedish history.

Drottningholm (p108)

A Renaissance-inspired summer palace.

Moderna Museet (p58)

Modern art, Scandinavian-style.

Fotografiska (p70)

Super-stylish photography museum.

Stockholm Archipelago (p120)

Boating around scenic rocky isles.

Stockholm
Local Life

*Local experiences and hidden gems
to help you uncover the real city*

Once you've checked the must-see sights off your list, it's time to experience Stockholm local-style. Be warned: there will be shopping involved. And parks. And bars – don't forget the bars.

Norrmalm Shopping
(p38)

☑ High-fashion boutiques ☑ Beautiful architecture

Escape to Djurgården
(p60)

☑ Verdant parks
☑ Quiet pathways

Bar-Hopping in Södermalm (p72)

☑ Characterful bars ☑ People-watching

Opulent Östermalm (p86)

☑ Eating and drinking ☑ Elegant boulevards

Other great places to experience the city like a local:

Stampen (p34)

Djurgården island (p66)

Lisa Larsson Second Hand (p80)

Nightlife around Östermalmstorg (p93)

Hit the urban beach at Smedsuddsbadet (p107)

Street eats in Kungsholmen (p104)

Park life in Vasaparken (p116)

Tennstopet (p119)

Gärdet & Ladugårdsgärdet Museums (p96)

☑ Excellent museums ☑ Parklike setting

Stockholm
Day Planner

Day One

Start early and beat the crowds to Gamla Stan. Fortify yourself with a coffee and pastry, then tour the royal palace, **Kungliga Slottet** (p24). The tour includes three other museums – the Museum Tre Kronor, devoted to Stockholm's original castle; the Royal Treasury; and Gustav III's Antikmuseum – all worth a look. Allow two or three hours to see everything.

After that, you'll need lunch: head for the veggie buffet at **Hermitage** (p32). Walk it off with a leisurely stroll from Gamla Stan across Norrbro and along the water's edge to the footbridge, called Skeppsholmsbron, which crosses to the island of Skeppsholmen. Here you can visit the contemporary-art powerhouse that is **Moderna Museet** (p58), then stop in for something completely different – 1000 years of Swedish architecture on display next door at **ArkDes** (p66).

Afterwards, walk back over the footbridge and into Norrmalm to settle in for a drink at **Berns Salonger** (p46). For dinner, make your way to **Grands Verandan** (p45) at the Grand Hôtel, for the famous Swedish smörgåsbord.

Day Two

On your second day, it's time to check a couple of Djurgården favourites off the list. First, spend a few hours exploring **Skansen** (p52), the open-air museum that calls itself 'Sweden in miniature'. Be sure to see the animals at the Nordic zoo, and don't miss the glassblowers' cottage. You could spend the day here, but there's more to see!

Venture further onto Djurgården for lunch at the gorgeous **Rosendals Trädgårdskafe** (p66), then backtrack to the amazing **Vasamuseet** (p56), a purpose-built museum dedicated to the battleship *Vasa*, which sunk on its maiden voyage in 1628. The multimedia displays here should keep you occupied for at least an hour or two. If you have time afterwards, pop next door to the **Spritmuseum** (p63) to get the low-down on the complicated history and social significance of booze in Sweden.

Take the ferry from Djurgården across to Norrmalm (summer only...or it's an easy walk) and make your way towards Stureplan, in Östermalm. Have an elegant dinner at the seafood-savvy **Sturehof** (p91), and drinks in its tiny, exclusive back bar, before exploring the surrounding clubs, including **Sturecompagniet** (p92) and **Spy Bar** (p92).

Short on time?
We've arranged Stockholm's must-sees into these day-by-day itineraries to make sure you see the very best of the city in the time you have available.

Day Three

☀ Three days in Stockholm will give you enough time to explore the city's fun southern neighbourhood, Södermalm, packed with shops and galleries and hipster hang-outs. Start at the brilliant photography gallery **Fotografiska** (p70) – you can grab a coffee and snack here too. From here, take the stairs up the cliffs to the Söder heights for killer views over the city.

☼ Grab lunch at **Hermans Trädgårdscafé** (p76), then walk back down the steep cobbled streets to Götgatan, Södermalm's main street, and follow it south to Medborgarplatsen. This is the neighbourhood's central square – there's always something going on here. Continue along the main drag, turning left onto Folkungagatan for the pubs and cafes of 'SoFo' (South of Folkungagatan).

☾ After dinner at **Chutney** (p76), aim for lovely, tree-lined Mariatorget, where you can sit with a drink outside the Rival Hotel, or continue walking north until you reach tiny Monteliusvägen, a footpath as much as a street, which offers another set of amazing views over Stockholm (particularly lovely at sunset). Beers at **Akkurat** (p79) await.

Day Four

☀ On day four, start with a tour of **Stadshuset** (p100), the surprisingly pretty City Hall, just across the bridge from Centralstationen on the island of Kungsholmen – also a nice neighbourhood to idly wander, if you're inspired to roam after your tour. Alternatively, if the weather is warm, bring swimwear and soak up the sun on the Stadshuset terrace like the locals.

☼ Next, hop on the tunnelbana to Östermalm for lunch at **Lisa Elmqvist** (p91) inside the fabulous **Östermalms Saluhall** (p90), where you can browse for speciality foods to take home as gifts (if they last that long). Afterwards, school yourself on Viking lore at **Historiska Museet** (p84), where displays include everything from skulls and armour to ancient coins and elaborate gold-filigree necklaces. Next up is a visit to **Svenskt Tenn** (p93) for a thoroughly impressive lesson in the fundamentals of Swedish interior design.

☾ Treat yourself to a top-flight dinner at **Ekstedt** (p90) or **Gastrologik** (p90), two of Stockholm's best restaurants, then boot it back to Norrmalm for cocktails and clubbing at **East** (p46) and **Café Opera** (p46).

Need to Know

For more information, see Survival Guide (p145)

Currency
Krona (kr)

Language
Swedish

Visas
Citizens of EU countries can enter Sweden with a passport. Visitors from Australia, New Zealand, Canada and the US can stay in Sweden without a visa for up to 90 days. Some nationalities need a Schengen visa in advance, good for 90 days.

Money
ATMs are widely available. Credit cards are accepted in most hotels and restaurants.

Mobile Phones
Most mobile phones work in Sweden, though often with hefty roaming fees. Local SIM cards also work in most phones, with the benefit of a local number and no roaming charges; ask your provider to unlock your phone for international travel.

Time
Central European Time (GMT/UTC plus one hour)

Tipping
Tipping is rare and usually reserved for good restaurant service (a 10–15% tip is customary). Tipping taxi drivers is optional, but most people add an extra 10–20kr.

① Before You Go

Your Daily Budget

Budget: Less than 1000kr
▶ Dorm bed or camping site: 250–650kr
▶ Fast-food lunch or sandwich: 65–99kr
▶ 24-hour bus and metro ticket: 120kr
▶ Museum admission: 100–150kr

Midrange: 1000–2000kr
▶ Double room: 1000–1600kr
▶ Restaurant meal: 185–200kr
▶ Happy-hour drink: 35–95kr

Top End: More than 2000kr
▶ Double room: 1600–2600kr
▶ Upscale dinner and drinks: 350–650kr
▶ Taxi from airport: 500kr

Useful Websites

Visit Stockholm (www.visitstockholm.com/en) Official visitor-info site.

Stockholm Public Transport (www.sl.se/en) Good info in English, including a trip planner.

Lonely Planet (www.lonelyplanet.com/sweden) Destination information, hotel bookings, traveller forum and more.

Advance Planning

Three months before Reserve a table at a top restaurant; book big-ticket excursions (Göta Canal).

One month before Make reservations for popular activities (kayak tours, walking tours); book tickets to performances (theatre, live music).

One week before Reserve train seats and long-distance buses.

② Arriving in Stockholm

From Stockholm Arlanda Airport

Flights to Stockholm generally land at Arlanda Airport, 45km north of the city. Terminals 2 and 5 are for international flights; 3 and 4 are domestic (there is no Terminal 1). There are car hire desks at the airport.

Arlanda Express (www.arlandaexpress.com; Centralstation; one way adult/child 280/150kr, 2 adults one way in summer 350kr; 🚆Centralen) trains between the airport and Centralstationen run every 10 to 15 minutes from 5am to 12.30am (less frequently after 9pm), taking 20 minutes.

Flygbussarna (www.flygbussarna.se; Cityterminalen; 🚆Centralen) buses run to/from Cityterminalen from stop 11 in Terminal 5 every 10 to 15 minutes (adult/child one way 119/99kr, 40 minutes).

Airport Cab (📞08-25 25 25; www.airportcab.se), **Sverige Taxi** (📞020-20 20 20; www.sverigetaxi.se) and **Taxi Stockholm** (📞15 00 00; www.taxistockholm.se) are reliable taxi services.

From Cityterminalen

Local buses go from here into Stockholm's various neighbourhoods; figure 20 minutes to downtown (85kr).

From Centralstationen

Local buses head to Stockholm's neighbourhoods from here; around one hour 20 minutes to downtown (159kr).

③ Getting Around

Storstockholms Lokaltrafik (SL; 📞08-600 10 00; www.sl.se; Centralstationen; 🕒SL Center Sergels Torg 7am-6.30pm Mon-Fri, 10am-5pm Sat & Sun, inside Centralstationen 6.30am-11.45pm Mon-Sat, from 7am Sun) runs the city's tunnelbana (metro), trains and buses.

Ⓜ Metro

Stockholm's fast, efficient underground Tunnelbana metro system connects various neighbourhoods.

🚌 Bus

The city bus system, using the same tickets/passes as the tunnelbana, is extensive. You must have your ticket or pass before boarding.

🚲 Cycling

Stockholm City Bikes (www.citybikes.se; 3-day/season card 165/300kr) has self-service bicycle-hire stands across the city.

🚊 Tram

Trams run between Norrmalmstorg and Skansen, passing most attractions on Djurgården.

🚕 Taxi

Taxis are readily available but fees are unregulated – check for a meter or arrange the fare first.

⛴ Ferry

In summer, ferries are the best way to get to Djurgården, and they serve the archipelago year-round.

Stockholm Neighbourhoods

Vasastan (p112)
Find some of the city's best restaurants in this no-nonsense neighbourhood.

Kungsholmen (p98)
Humble 'hood with a friendly vibe and great places to swim.

⊙ **Top Sights**
Stadshuset

Stadshuset ⊙

Norrmalm (p36)
Eat, shop and play in the bustling heart of the city.

Worth a Trip
⊙ **Top Sights**
Millesgården
Drottningholm
Stockholm Archipelago

Södermalm (p68)
The arty part of town, ultra-stylish but casual and fun.

⊙ **Top Sights**
Fotografiska

Östermalm (p82)
Dress up and scope out the beautiful people over a flute of bubbly.

⊙ Top Sights

Historiska Museet

Djurgården & Skeppsholmen (p50)
A parklike oasis with most of the city's best museums.

⊙ Top Sights

Skansen

Vasamuseet

Moderna Museet

⊙ Historiska Museet

⊙ Vasamuseet   ⊙ Skansen

⊙ Kungliga Slottet

⊙ Moderna Museet

Fotografiska ⊙

Gamla Stan (p22)
A medieval labyrinth of cobblestone streets and saffron-hued buildings.

⊙ Top Sights

Kungliga Slottet

Explore
Stockholm

Gamla Stan (p22)
SCANRAIL1/SHUTTERSTOCK ©

Explore

Gamla Stan

The old town is Stockholm's historic and geographic heart. Here, cobblestone streets wriggle past Renaissance churches, baroque palaces and medieval squares. Spice-coloured buildings sag like wizened old men, and narrow lanes harbour everything from dusty toy shops to candlelit cafes. Västerlånggatan is the area's nerve centre, a busy thoroughfare lined with galleries, eateries and souvenir shops.

The Sights in a Day

☼ Fuel up with a decadent pastry and coffee at **Grillska Husets Konditori** (p34), then hop over to **Kungliga Slottet** (p24), the royal palace, to get in with an early tour group. After the tour, make sure to peek into the Museum Tre Kronor in the basement, as well as the Royal Treasury and Gustav III's Antikmuseum. If you finish up around noon you'll catch the impressive Changing of the Guard, with its fanfare and marching band.

☼ Wander down to Stora Nygatan for a healthy buffet lunch at **Hermitage** (p32), then stroll along towards Riddarholmen to admire the lovely iron-spired **Riddarholmskyrkan** (p30) and its surrounding islet. Crossing back over to Gamla Stan, take a look inside **Storkyrkan** (p32; pictured left), then settle in for some inspiration and innovation at the **Nobelmuseet** (p30).

☾ After all that museum-going, you'll want to sit for a moment with a latte or hot cocoa and do some hardcore people-watching from the terrace of **Chokladkoppen** (p32). Then wander some shopping streets or grab a brew or two at **Monks Porter House** (p35), before dinner at the traditional **Fem Små Hus** (p34) near the Royal Palace.

◉ **Top Sight**

Kungliga Slottet (p24)

♥ **Best of Stockholm**

Eating

Kryp In (p32)

Hermitage (p32)

Magnus Ladulås (p34)

Fem Små Hus (p34)

Cafes

Grillska Husets Konditori (p34)

Chokladkoppe (p32)

Museums & Galleries

Nobelmuseet (p30)

Medeltidsmuseet (p30)

Live Music

Stampen (p34)

Design

Studio Lena M (p35)

E Torndahl (p35)

Getting There

Ⓜ **Metro** (Tunnelbana) Gamla Stan, Slussen

🚌 **Bus** 43, 46, 55, 59 to Slottsbacken

🚶 **Walk** The old town is an easy stroll from the city centre

Top Sights
Kungliga Slottet

Stockholm's imposing 608-room royal palace – the largest in the world still in use – houses some beautiful examples of Swedish baroque and rococo interiors. The palace dominates tiny Gamla Stan and was built on the ruins of Tre Kronor castle, most of which burned to the ground in 1697. The north wing survived and was incorporated into the new building. Designed by the court architect Nicodemus Tessin the Younger, it took 57 years to complete. The royal family has lived here since 1754. Guided tours make Swedish history entertaining.

Map p28, E2

www.theroyalpalace.se

Slottsbacken; adult/child 160/80kr,

9am-5pm Jul & Aug, 10am-5pm May-Jun & Sep, 10am-4pm Tue-Sun Oct-Apr

43, 46, 55, 59 Slottsbacken, Gamla Stan

Changing of the Guard

Changing of the Guard

It's worth timing your visit to see the Changing of the Guard, which takes place in the outer courtyard at 12.15pm Monday to Saturday and 1.15pm on Sundays and public holidays May through August, but only on Wednesday, Saturday, Sunday and public holidays September to April.

Museum Tre Kronor

This museum displays the foundations of 13th-century defensive walls and items rescued from the castle during the 1697 fire. It describes how the fire started (a watchman was off flirting with a kitchen maid) and vividly explains the meaning of 'run the gauntlet' (which in 1697 was the punishment for flirting with kitchen maids while fire destroyed the castle).

Gustav III's State Bedchamber

King Gustav III, whose efforts to reconsolidate power for the throne in the early part of his reign made him unpopular with the nobility, died here in 1792 – a full 13 days after an assassin shot him during a masquerade ball. He survived just long enough to keep up appearances and suppress the attempted coup.

Silver Throne

Queen Christina's silver throne, in the Hall of State, was rescued from the Tre Kronor fire. It was a gift to the queen from Swedish statesman Magnus Gabriel de la Gardie (son of Ebba Brahe, who had an affair with King Gustavus Adolphus).

Karl XI Gallery

One of the prettiest rooms in the palace, and still used today for royal functions, the decadent Karl XI Gallery was inspired by Versailles' Hall of Mirrors and is considered the finest example of Swedish late baroque.

☑ Top Tips

▶ Beat the crowds: for the best experience, arrive right when the palace opens.

▶ Free 45-minute tours in English are well worth taking – check timetables online for the current schedule.

▶ Admission to the palace also includes the nearby Museum Tre Kronor, the Royal Treasury and the Antikmuseum.

▶ Tickets are valid for seven days.

▶ The apartments are occasionally closed for royal business; closures are noted on the website.

✗ Take a Break

From June to late August, a small cafe with outdoor tables in the castle's inner courtyard serves light lunches, coffee and pastries. Kungliga Slottet is also a cobblestone's throw from the cosy Chokladkoppen (p32).

Understand
The Bernadottes

When King Gustav IV Adolf was forced to abdicate the throne after losing Finland, the Swedish nobles had to find a replacement; there was no heir. So a Baron Mörner invited one of Napoleon's marshals, Jean-Baptiste Bernadotte (1763–1844), to take the Swedish throne. He agreed, changing his name to Karl Johan, ruling for 26 years and starting the Bernadotte dynasty that still holds the throne today.

Royal Treasury

The Royal Treasury (Skattkammaren) contains ceremonial crowns, sceptres and other regalia of the Swedish monarchy, including Lovisa Ulrika's crown, a 1696 baptismal font (still used today for royal baptisms), tapestries rescued from the 1697 fire and a 16th-century sword that belonged to Gustav Vasa.

Antikmuseum

Gustav III's Museum of Antiquities (summer only) displays sculpture mostly collected by King Gustav III during his Italian journeys (the requisite 'grand tour') in the 1780s. For most of the Swedish public, this was a first glimpse of classical sculpture. The galleries were renovated starting in the 1950s in order to keep the collection safely in its original home.

Royal Chapel

A chapel has stood in the royal palace since the 1200s, but this version of it – dating from the palace reopening in 1754 – was a 50-year project, overseen by Nicodemus Tessin the Younger.

Kungliga Slottet

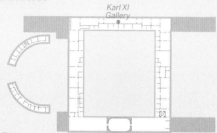

Karl XI
Gallery

First Floor

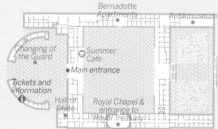

Bernadotte
Apartments

Antikmuseum

Changing of
the Guard

Summer
Cafe

Main entrance

Tickets and
information

Hall of
State

Royal Chapel &
entrance to
Royal Treasury

Ground Floor

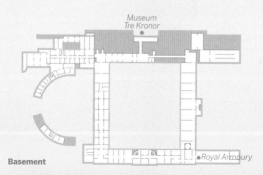

Museum
Tre Kronor

Royal Armoury

Basement

A **B** **C** **D**

1

Centralbron

Norra
Järnvägsbron

Vasabron

Strömsborg

Riksbron

Strömparterren
Helgeandsholmen

Riksdagshuset
◉ 5

Riksgatan

Bankkajen Stallbron

2

Norra
Riddarholmshamnen

Arkivgatan

Riddarhuskajen

Rådhusgränd

Riddarhusgränd

Riddarhuset

Mynttorget

Myntgatan

Riddarhustorget

Storkyrkobrinken

RIDDARHOLMEN

Evert
Taubes
Terrass

Wrangelska
Palatset

Birger
Jarls Torg

Wrangelska Backen

Stora
Gråmunkegränd

Prästgatan

8
Gåsgränd
Överskärargränd

3

Norrström

4 ◉

Riddarholmskyrkan

15
⚲

Lilla Nygatan

Yxsmedsgränd

Stora Nygatan

Mälardrottningen
Hotel &
Restaurant

Södra Riddarholmshamnen

Munkbroleden

Munkbrogatan

Käkbrinken

Schönfelts Gränd

4

Riddarfjärden

Södra Järnvägsbron

Ⓜ Gamla
Stan

Tyska
Brinken

Mälartorget

5

◎N 0 ⊨▬▬▬▬▬▬⊨ 200 m
0 ⊨▬▬▬▬▬⊨ 0.1 miles

Södra
Järnvägsbron

Centralbron

E **⊙3** Medeltidsmuseet

Norrbro

Strömbron **F**

Norrström **G**

Nationalmuseum **H**

Slottskajen

Skeppsholmsbron

Skeppsbrokajen

Mynttorget

Kungliga Slottet

Yttre Borggården ⊙

Royal Armoury **2⊙**

Slottsbacken

7⊙ Storkyrkan

Telegrafgränd

Trädgårdsgatan

Nobelmuseet **⊙1**

Bollhusgränd

Bredgränd

ⓘ Tourist Center
Köpmangatan

Kråkgränd
⊗12 Nygränd

Stortorget
⊗14 Gamla Stan

Brunnsgränd

⊗11

Skottgränd Gamla Stans Bryggeri

17ⓐ Kindstugatan

Skomakargatan

Svartmangatan

Själagårdsgatan

Baggensgatan

Österlånggatan

Drakens Gränd

13

Västerlånggatan

Prästgatan

Tyska Skolgränd

⊗ Johannesgränd

16

Mårten Trotzigs Gränd

Packhusgränd

Ⓢunstedts Gränd

Kornhamnstorg

⊙6 Järntorget

Munkbroleden

Triewaldsgränd

Järntorgsgatan

Tullgränd

Norra Bankogränd

Skeppsbron

Skeppsbrokajen

Strömmen

Norra Dryckesgränd

Slussplan

Riddarfjärden

For reviews see	
⊙ Top Sights	p24
⊙ Sights	p30
⊗ Eating	p32
⊙ Drinking	p35
ⓐ Shopping	p35

Sights

Nobelmuseet
MUSEUM

1 Map p28, E3

Nobelmuseet presents the history of the Nobel Prize, with a focus on the intellectual and cultural aspects of invention. It's a slick space with fascinating displays, including short films on the theme of creativity, interviews with laureates like Ernest Hemingway and Martin Luther King, and cafe chairs signed by the visiting prize recipients (flip them over to see!). (☑08-54 43 18 00; www.nobelmuseet.se; Stortorget; adult/child 120kr/free; ⏱9am-8pm Jun-Aug, shorter hours rest of year; 🚌53, 🚇Gamla Stan)

Royal Armoury
MUSEUM

2 Map p28, F2

The Royal Armoury is housed in the cellar vaults of the palace but has separate hours. It's a family attic of sorts, crammed with engrossing memorabilia spanning more than 500 years of royal childhoods, coronations, weddings and murders. Meet Gustav II Adolf's stuffed battle steed, Streiff;

---

see the costume Gustav III wore to the masquerade ball on the night he was shot in 1792; or let the kids try on a suit of armour in the playroom. (Livrustkammaren; ☑08-402 30 30; www.livrustkammaren.se; Slottsbacken 3; admission free; ⏱10am-5pm, to 6pm Jul-Aug; 🚌43, 46, 55, 59 Slottsbacken, 🚇Gamla Stan)

Medeltidsmuseet
MUSEUM

3 Map p28, E1

Tucked beneath the bridge that links Gamla Stan and Norrmalm, this child-friendly museum was established when construction workers preparing to build a car park here in the late 1970s unearthed foundations from the 1530s. The ancient walls were preserved as found, and a museum was built around them. The circular plan leads visitors through faithful reconstructions of typical homes, markets and workshops from medieval Stockholm. Tickets are valid for one year. (Medieval Museum; www.medeltidsmuseet.stockholm.se; Strömparterren; admission free; ⏱noon-5pm Tue-Sun, to 8pm Wed; 🚌62, 65, Gustav Adolfs torg)

Riddarholmskyrkan
CHURCH

4 Map p28, B3

The strikingly beautiful Riddarholmskyrkan, on the equally pretty and under-visited islet of Riddarholmen, was built by Franciscan monks in the late 13th century. It has been the royal necropolis since the burial of Magnus Ladulås in 1290, and is home to the armorial glory of the Seraphim knightly

Riksdagshuset (Swedish Parliament building)

order. There's a guided tour in English at noon (included with admission) and occasional concerts. Holiday closures are frequent; check the website for updates. Admission fee is by credit card only. (Riddarholmen Church; ☎08-402 61 30; www.kungahuset.se; Riddarholmen; adult/child 50/25kr; ⏱10am-5pm mid-May–mid-Sep; ⛴3, 53 Riddarhustorget, 🚇Gamla Stan)

Riksdagshuset NOTABLE BUILDING

5 ◎ Map p28, D1

Technically situated on Helgeandsholmen, the little island in the middle of Norrström, rather than on Gamla Stan, the Swedish Parliament building is an unexpected pleasure to visit. The building consists of two parts: the older front section (facing downstream) dates from the early 20th century, but the other more-modern part contains the current debating chamber. Tours of the building offer a compelling glimpse into the Swedish system of consensus-building government. (Swedish Parliament; ☎020-34 80 00; www.riksdagen.se; Riksgatan 3; admission free; ⏱1hr tours in English noon, 1pm, 2pm & 3pm Mon-Fri mid-Jun–mid-Aug, 1.30pm Sat & Sun Oct–mid-Jun; ⛴3, 59, Riddarhustorget, 🚇Gamla Stan, T-Centralen)

Mårten Trotzigs Gränd AREA

6 ◎ Map p28, F4

This tiny alley in Gamla Stan is Stockholm's narrowest street and a popular spot for a photo op. (🚇Gamla Stan)

Storkyrkan
CHURCH

7 Map p28, E2

The one-time venue for royal weddings and coronations, Storkyrkan is both Stockholm's oldest building (consecrated in 1306) and its cathedral. Behind a baroque facade, the Gothic-baroque interior includes extravagant royal-box pews designed by Nicodemus Tessin the Younger, as well as German Berndt Notke's dramatic sculpture *St George and the Dragon,* commissioned by Sten Sture the Elder to commemorate his victory over the Danes in 1471. Keep an eye out for posters and handbills advertising music performances here. (Great Church; www.stockholmsdomkyrkoforsamling.se; Trångsund 1; adult/child 60kr/free; ⏲9am-4pm, to 6pm Jun-Aug; 🚇Gamla Stan)

Eating

Hermitage
VEGETARIAN $$

8 Map p28, D3

Herbivores love Hermitage for its simple, tasty vegetarian buffet, easily one of the best bargains in Gamla Stan. Salad, homemade bread, tea and coffee are included in the price. Pro tip: don't miss the drawers of hot food hiding under the main buffet tabletop. Vegan fare is also available, including cakes. (www.hermitage.gastrogate.com; Stora Nygatan 11; buffet weekday/weekend 130/140kr; ⏲11am-8pm Mon-Fri, noon-8pm Sat & Sun, to 9pm Jun-Aug; 🖊; 🚇Gamla Stan)

Kryp In
SWEDISH $$$

9 Map p28, E3

Small but perfectly formed, this spot wows diners with creative takes on traditional Swedish dishes. Expect the likes of salmon carpaccio, Kalix roe, reindeer roast or gorgeous, spirit-warming saffron aioli shellfish stew. The service is seamless and the atmosphere classy without being stuffy. The three-course set menu (455kr) is superb. Book ahead. (📞08-20 88 41; www.restaurangkrypin.nu; Prästgatan 17; lunch mains 135-168kr, dinner mains 198-290kr; ⏲5-11pm Mon-Fri, noon-4pm & 5-11pm Sat & Sun; 🛜; 🚇Gamla Stan)

Chokladkoppen
CAFE $

10 Map p28, E3

Arguably Stockholm's best-loved cafe, hole-in-the-wall Chokladkoppen sits slap bang on the old town's enchanting main square. It's an atmospheric spot with a sprawling terrace and pocket-sized interior with low-beamed ceilings, custard-coloured walls and edgy artwork. The menu includes savoury treats like broccoli-and-blue-cheese pie and scrumptious cakes. (www.chokladkoppen.se; Stortorget 18; cakes & coffees from 35kr, mains 85-125kr; ⏲9am-11pm Jun-Aug, shorter hours rest of year; 🛜; 🚇Gamla Stan)

Under Kastanjen
SWEDISH $$

11 Map p28, F3

This has to be just about the most picturesque corner of Gamla Stan, with tables set on a cobbled square under

Understand

Government & Politics

The current king of Sweden, Karl XVI Gustaf, is the seventh ruler of the Bernadotte dynasty. He became crown prince at age four and king at 27 (in 1973). He met Queen Silvia, a German-Brazilian who was neither a royal nor a member of the nobility, at the Munich Olympic Games in 1972. Their eldest daughter, Crown Princess Victoria, will be the next monarch. (Since 1980 it has been Swedish policy that the first-born is heir to the throne regardless of gender.)

The king is head of state and an important figure, but apolitical, with mostly ceremonial and ambassadorial duties. Sweden is governed by Parliament, with elections held every four years. Despite the country's middle-way steadiness over the long term, recent changes in the economy and the political mood have led some to question their assumptions. For decades Sweden was viewed by left-leaning outsiders as an almost utopian model of a socialist state, a successful experiment that gave hope to progressives everywhere. This is still more or less true. But as the country has grown, it has had to adjust to modern realities – both economic and sociopolitical – and some cracks have begun to appear in the facade.

The Social Democrats, who held a majority of the government for most of the past 85 years (and therefore shaped national policy, most notably the famous 'cradle to grave' welfare state), have seen their influence wane in recent years.

The 2010 election saw the Social Democrats' worst results since 1921: they won just over 30% of the seats in Parliament. The Alliance Party won a second term (173 of the 349 seats), but unemployment was high and by 2012 the Social Democrats had regained some favour.

By the September 2014 election, the Social Democrats were back: Alliance Party leader Fredrik Reinfeldt lost his bid for a third term, and Social Democrats leader Stefan Löfven became prime minister. The biggest factor in the election was the right-wing nationalist Sweden Democrats party, which saw twice the support it had previously – going from 20 to 49 seats, making it the third-largest party in Parliament. This immediately began to create friction, as the other parties have been reluctant to cooperate with the Sweden Democrats.

a beautiful chestnut tree surrounded by ochre and yellow storybook houses. Enjoy classic Swedish dishes like homemade meatballs with mashed potato; the downstairs wine bar has a veritable Spanish bodega feel with its whitewashed brick arches and moody lighting. (☎08-21 50 04; www.underkastanjen.se; Kindstugatan 1, Gamla Stan; mains 182-289kr, dagens lunch 105kr; ⏲8am-11pm Mon-Fri, 9am-11pm Sat, 9am-9pm Sun; 📶; Ⓜ Gamla Stan)

Fem Små Hus — SWEDISH **$$$**

12 Map p28, F3

Fem Små Hus offers the perfect combination of authentic historical setting with traditional cuisine, just a short walk from the Royal Palace in the heart of the old town. The menu features Swedish classics with a French touch – think reindeer fillets with port wine sauce, seared Arctic char, Swedish farm chicken confit – served in 17th-century vaulted cellars. (☎08-10 87 75; www.femsmahus.se; Nygränd 10; mains 205-410kr; ⏲11.30am-11pm Mon-Tu, to midnight Wed-Fri, 1pm-midnight Sat, 1-11pm Sun; Ⓜ Gamla Stan)

Local Life

Stompin' at Stampen

Stampen (Map p28, D3, ☎08-20 57 93; www.stampen.se; Stora Nygatan 5; cover free-200kr; ⏲5pm-1am Tue-Fri & Sun, 2pm-1am Sat; Ⓜ Gamla Stan) is one of Stockholm's music-club stalwarts, swinging to live jazz and blues six nights a week. The free blues jam (currently on Sundays) pulls everyone from local noodlers to the odd music legend.

Magnus Ladulås — SWEDISH **$$$**

13 Map p28, F4

Named after King Magnus III, Restaurang Magnus Ladulås is housed on the site of a 16th-century eatery. Tables hug sloped ceilings in this authentic and intimate setting where the menu is built around Swedish classics – think meatballs with potatoes and lingon, seafood stew, or pike-perch with roe and lobster sauce. (☎08-21 19 57; http://magnusladulas.se; Österlånggatan 26; mains 195-289kr; ⏲11am-10pm Mon-Thu, to 11pm Fri, 1-11pm Sat, to 8pm Sun; Ⓜ Gamla Stan)

Grillska Husets Konditori — BAKERY, CAFE **$**

14 Map p28, E3

The cafe and bakery run by Stockholms Stadsmission, the chain of secondhand charity shops, is an excellent spot for a sweet treat or a traditional shrimp sandwich, especially when warm weather allows for seating at the outdoor tables in Gamla Stan's main square. There's a bakery shop attached, selling goodies and rustic breads to take away. (☎08-68 42 33 64; www.stadsmissionen.se/vad-vi-gor/grillska-huset; Stortorget 3; mains 90-125kr, lunch special 125kr; ⏲10am-8pm Mon, to 9pm Tue-Sat, 11am-8pm Sun; Ⓜ Gamla Stan)

Drinking

Monks Porter House
PUB

15 Map p28, C3

This cavernous brewpub has an epic beer list, including 56 taps, many of which are made here or at the Monks microbrewery in Vasastan. Everything we tried was delicious, especially the Monks Orange Ale – your best bet is to ask the bartender for a recommendation (or a taste). Check online for beer-tasting events. (☎08-23 12 12; www.monkscafe.se; Munkbron 11; ☉6pm-1am Tue-Sat; ☒Gamla Stan)

Shopping

E Torndahl
DESIGN

16 🔒 Map p28, E4

This spacious design shop, run by the women of the Torndahl family since 1864, is a calm and civilised oasis on busy Västerlånggatan, offering jewellery, textiles and clever Scandinavian household objects. (www.etorndahl.se; Västerlånggatan 63; ☉10am-8pm; ☒Gamla Stan)

Chokladkoppen cafe (p32)

Studio Lena M
GIFTS & SOUVENIRS

17 🔒 Map p28, E3

This tiny, dimly lit shop is chock full of adorable prints and products featuring the distinctive graphic design work of Lena M. It's a great place to find a unique – and uniquely Swedish – gift to bring home, or even just a cute postcard. (www.studiolenam.wordpress.com; Kindstugan 14; ☉10am-6pm, to 5pm Sat; ☒Gamla Stan)

Explore

Norrmalm

The modern heart of the city, Norrmalm is where most visits to Stockholm begin: it's home to the main train and bus stations, Centralstationen and Cityterminalen respectively. It's also where you'll find the highest concentration of schmancy retail boutiques, glamorous bars and restaurants, hotels from functional to fabulous, and noteworthy cultural institutions.

The Sights in a Day

☼ Start your day with a dose of fine art, courtesy of the **Nationalmuseum** (p42), whose collections include fine art from around Europe as well as a great stash of Scandinavian design objects. Afterwards, get ready for some serious interior-decorating voyeurism with a tour of the **Hallwylska Museet** (p42), the former home of a wealthy count and countess who collected objets d'art with the intent of eventually displaying them to the public.

☼ Next up, change centuries with a visit to the very hip **Wetterling Gallery** (p42). This is where up-and-coming Stockholm artists – painters, photographers and new-media protagonists – strut their stuff.

☾ Wrap up the afternoon at the **Medelhavsmuseet** (p42), filled with fascinating artefacts and artwork, notably Egyptian lore and ancient Greek and Roman sculpture. There's a great cafe here if you're still hungry, or head for the ultimate smörgåsbord dinner at **Grands Verandan** (p45). Clubby nights await at **Café Opera** (p46) or **Berns Salonger** (p46).

For a local's day shopping in Norrmalm, see p38.

 Local Life

 Best of Stockholm

Getting There

Ⓜ **Metro** (Tunnelbana) T-Centralen, Kungsträdgården

🚌 **Bus** Cityterminalen, Norrmalmstorg, Sergels Torg

🚊 **Tram** 7

Local Life
Norrmalm Shopping

Ever wondered how Stockholmers manage to look so fashionable all the time? Shopping is a sport here, and Norrmalm is one of the best places to do it well. Its chic storefronts peddle everything from traditional handmade crafts to fine crystal, outdoors equipment to the most exclusive high-fashion brands. And a good stretch of the district is pedestrian-only, so you can focus on the task at hand.

❶ Norrmalmstorg

Start your mission at the heart of the district, the wide-open square of Norrmalmstorg. At its easternmost edge you'll find the epitome of Stockholm cool, **Acne** (☎08-611 64 11; www.acne studios.com; Norrmalmstorg 2; ⏰10am-7pm Mon-Fri, to 5pm Sat, noon-4pm Sun; 🚇Östermalmstorg), with a shop that closely resembles a fashion museum. In the same block you'll find the impossible-to-resist **Marimekko** (☎08-440 32 75;

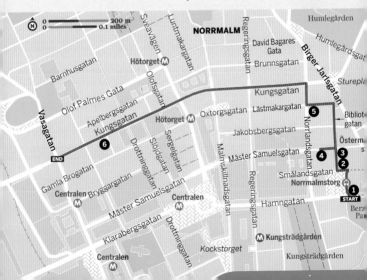

www.marimekko.com; Norrmalmstorg 4;
⏱10am-7pm Mon-Fri, to 5pm Sat; 🚇Öster-
malmstorg), purveyors of ultra-fun
patterned textiles. This Finnish textile
company plasters almost everything
with its iconic prints, from towels,
cups and coasters to notebooks, bags,
napkins and clothes.

❷ Biblioteksgatan

At the north end of Norrmalmstorg is
this pedestrianised shopping street,
lined wall-to-wall with hot brand
names. Right on the corner is an
outlet of the groundbreaking Swedish
fashion designer **Filippa K** (www.filippa-
k.com; Biblioteksgatan 2; ⏱10am-7pm Mon-
Sat, noon-5pm Sun; 🚇Östermalmstorg).

❸ Mäster Samuelsgatan

This street, which crosses Biblioteksgatan, is home to a dense population
of big-name fashion. Off to the right is
Whyred (📞08-660 01 70; www.whyred.se;
Mäster Samuelsgatan 3; ⏱10am-7pm Mon-
Fri, to 5pm Sat, noon-4pm Sun; 🚇Östermalm-
storg), beloved for men's sweaters and
women's shoes, among other things;
next to that is the relatively new **BLK
DNM** (📞08-678 83 00; www.blkdnm.com;
Mäster Samuelsgatan 1; 🚇Östermalmstorg),
with its painfully hip jackets and
other clothing by designer Johan
Lindeberg.

❹ Cow Parfymeri

A great place to pick up gifts to bring
home, **Cow Parfymeri** (📞08-611 15 04;
www.cowparfymeri.se; Mäster Samuelsgatan 9;
⏱11am-6pm Mon-Fri, to 4pm Sat; 🚇Öster-
malmstorg) is a cool cosmetics temple
with a trendsetting range of perfumes,
sticks and shades. Pick up rock-chic
cosmetics from Urban Decay and
Vincent Longo, or spray yourself silly
with hard-to-find fragrances from Paris
and New York.

❺ Espresso Stop

By now you're probably ready for a
break. The lovely **Bianchi Cafe &
Cycles** (📞08-611 21 00; www.bianchicafe
cycles.com; Norrlandsgatan 16; ⏱11am-10pm
Mon-Sat; 🚇Östermalmstorg) is an ideal
spot for an espresso and a pastry.

❻ Kungsgatan

You'll pass by all manner of retail
outlets here, both local and global,
including the fun outdoor market and
food hall at Hötorget. Several blocks
along, stop in at **Iris Hantverk** (📞08-21
47 26; Kungsgatan 55; ⏱10am-8pm Mon-Fri,
to 3pm Sat; 🚇T-Centralen, Hötorget) for
gorgeous handmade Swedish crafts:
expect impeccably made woodwork,
linens, textiles, candlesticks, soaps,
glassware and crafting books. Across
the street is **WESC** (📞08-21 25 15; www.
wesc.com; Kungsgatan 66; ⏱11am-6pm Mon-
Fri, 10am-4pm Sat; 🚇Hötorget), another
museumlike store carrying skate-
board-inspired fashion. This street-
smart label got started by dressing up
underground artists and muses. It has
since become one of Swedish fashion's
big guns, opening up stores from
Seoul to Beverly Hills.

Birger Jarlsgatan
Engelbrektsgatan
Humlegården
Kungliga Biblioteket
Engelbrektsplan
avid Bagares Gata
Sturegatan
Engelbrektsgatan
Blakegatan
Grev Turegatan

For reviews see

⊙	Sights	p42
✖	Eating	p43
◷	Drinking	p46
✿	Entertainment	p48
🛍	Shopping	p49

Kungsgatan
Norrlandsgatan
Stureplan
14
ÖSTERMALM
Ⓜ Östermalmstorg
15
Bibliteksgatan
Östermalmstorg
Hedvig Eleonora kyrka
Storgatan
Lästmakargatan
Jakobsbergsgatan
Ⓜ Östermalmstorg
Nybrogatan
Sibyllegatan
Armémuseum
Artillerigatan
Skeppargatan
🛍 25
10 ✖
Birger Jarlsgatan
Mäster Samuelsgatan
Smålandsgatan
Norrmalmstorg
Hallwylska Museet
Dramatiska teatern
Kungliga Hovstallet
Riddargatan
🛍 22
24 🛍
Norrmalmstorg ⊙ 5
Kaptensgatan
Greygatan
Hamngatan
Berzelii Park
Nybroplan
ungsträdgården
Ⓜ
9
Wetterling Gallery
Näckströmsgatan
Raoul Wallenbergs Torg
12
Strandvägen
Tram Line 7
Kocksgränd
Vastra Trädgårdsgatan
Kungsträdgården
Wahrendorffsgatan
Nybroviken
Strandvägen
Regeringsgatan
Jakobs Kyrka
Kungsträdgården
Ⓜ
Blasieholmsgatan
Greyvand
Djurgårdsfärjan Ferry (Summer Only)
Ladugårdslandsviken
Fredsgatan
Karl XII's Torg
11
13
17
Strömgatan
Stallgatan
8
Grand Hôtel Stockholm
Nybrokajen
Hovslagaregatan
ustav dolfs Torg
Södra Blasieholmshamnen
Norrbro
Norrström
Strömbron
Museiparken
Nationalmuseum
⊙ 1
Strömparteren
Museikajen
ksdagshuset

Sights

Nationalmuseum
MUSEUM

1 Map p40, G5

Sweden's largest art museum is home to the nation's collection of painting, sculpture, drawings, decorative arts and graphics from the Middle Ages to the present. (National Art Museum; www.national museum.se; Södra Blasieholmshamnen; 🚌65)

Wetterling Gallery
GALLERY

2 Map p40, E4

This cool gallery space at the edge of Kungsträdgården always has something interesting going on – usually a boundary-pushing contemporary painter, but there's also often photography or multimedia work, from big names (eg Frank Stella) to soon-to-be-big names. (📞08-10 10 09; www.wetterling gallery.com; Kungsträdgården 3; ⏰11am-5pm Wed-Fri, 1-4pm Sat; 🚇Kungsträdgården)

Kulturhuset
ARTS CENTRE

3 Map p40, D4

This architecturally divisive building, opened in 1974, is an arts hub, with a couple of galleries and workshops, a cinema, three restaurants, and libraries containing international periodicals, newspapers, books and an unusually good selection of graphic novels in many languages. It's home to Stadsteatern (the City Theatre), with performances in various-sized venues (mostly in Swedish). Stockholm's main visitor centre is also here, on the lower level. (📞tickets noon-5pm 08-50 62 02 00; www.kulturhusetstadsteatern.se; Sergels Torg; ⏰11am-5pm, some sections closed Mon; 🚻; 🚌52, 56, 59, 69, 91 Sergels Torg, 🚋7 Sergels Torg, 🚇T-Centralen)

Medelhavsmuseet
MUSEUM

4 Map p40, D5

Housed in an elegant Italianate building, Medelhavsmuseet lures history buffs with its Egyptian, Greek, Cypriot, Roman and Etruscan treasures. A large portion of the main hall is devoted to the Swedish expedition to Cyprus in 1927, which unearthed masses of well-preserved artefacts that are attractively displayed here. Don't miss the gleaming gold room, home to a 4th-century BC olive wreath made of gold. And in the basement: mummies! The attached Bagdad Cafe (open 11.30am to 1.30pm) has great food and atmosphere. (Museum of Mediterranean Antiquities; 📞010-456 12 98; www.medel-havsmuseet.se; Fredsgatan 2; admission free; ⏰noon-8pm Tue-Fri, to 5pm Sat & Sun; 🚇Centralen, Kungsträdgården)

Hallwylska Museet
MUSEUM

5 Map p40, F3

A private palace completed in 1898, Hallwylska Museet was once home to compulsive hoarder Wilhelmina von Hallwyl, who collected items as diverse as kitchen utensils, Chinese pottery, 17th-century paintings, silverware, sculpture and her children's teeth. In 1920 she and her husband donated the mansion and its

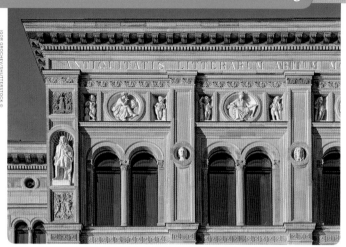

IGOR GROCHEV/SHUTTERSTOCK ©

Nationalmuseum (National Art Museum)

contents to the state. Guided tours in English take place at 12.30pm Tuesday through Sunday June through August (weekends only the rest of the year). The museum is not wheelchair accessible. (Hallwyl Collection; ☎08-402 30 99; www.hallwylskamuseet.se; Hamngatan 4; tours 40kr; ⏱10am-7pm Tue-Sun Jul-Aug, to 4pm rest of year; ⊠Östermalmstorg)

Sergels Torg SQUARE

6 ◎ Map p40, D3

Stockholm's living room, this circular square (which was undergoing major repairs on our last visit, but was still accessible to foot traffic) is a little on the grungy side, and you'll want to keep close tabs on your wallet, but it's a key transit hub as well as a great place to catch the pulse of the city. Something's always going on here, be it an impromptu classical music performance or a hundreds-strong political demonstration.

Eating

Rutabaga VEGETARIAN $$$

7 ✗ Map p40, F5

At Rutabaga, celebrity chef Mathias Dahlgren pushes vegetarian cuisine into the realm of art: the menu features vividly colourful salads and other unusual combinations (an egg-truffle-white-bean dish, a mango and

Understand

Swedish Design

- -

You don't have to spend much time window-shopping in this city to re-alise that Stockholm is a living museum of contemporary design. There are zero unstyled objects – no ordinary anything. From milk cartons by Tom Hedqvist to ballerina 'tutu' lamps by Jonas Bohlin and cute IKEA kitchen hooks, the everyday things you see around you here are object lessons in style and innovation. At the core of Swedish design – and architecture – is simple structural elegance above all. The characteristi-cally Swedish interests of nature and craft also inform contemporary design.

Democracy in a Flat-Pack

Seeking to bring simple, good design to the whole world, in an affordable way, Swedish company IKEA has had enormous influence, across Scan-dinavia and beyond. Ingvar Kamprad started the company in 1943 when he was 17 years old, creating cheap and innovative products born out of Swedish modern design – with the idea of the house as the starting point of good design, rather than the end. Today IKEA has stores in more than 50 countries, with new openings always on the agenda.

Where to Find It

There are many ways to immerse yourself in Swedish design and gain an appreciation for its history: one is simply to walk around the city with your eyes open. But it's also worthwhile to spend some time window-shopping, especially at landmark shops like Svenskt Tenn (p93) and Nordiska Galleriet (p93).

Department stores like NK (p49) are also great sources of the things everyday Swedes furnish their homes with. For something more akin to a history lesson, visit Nordiska Museet (p63) and its displays of design objects from throughout Swedish history. Or make a pilgrimage to some of the sleeker hotels, bars and restaurants in town – Sturehof (p91) was gussied up by Jonas Bohlin; Thomas Sandell did Café Opera (p46); and you can enjoy a smörgåsbord of interior designers at design-focused boutique hotels like the **Birger Jarl Hotel** (📞08-674 18 00; www.birgerjarl. se; Tulegatan 8; cabin r from 1190kr; s/d from 1200/1400kr; 🅿️🚗❄️@🛜; 🚌43 Tegnérgatan, 🚇Rådmansgatan).

mozzarella salad) which, as always, Dahlgren presents impeccably on the plate. Most dishes are meant for sharing (if you can bear to give any up). Closes in July. (☑08-679 35 84; www.mdghs.se; Södra Blasieholmshamnen 6, Grand Hôtel Stockholm; dishes 125-295kr; ⏱5pm-midnight Mon-Sat; 🚇Kungsträdgården)

Grands Verandan
SWEDISH $$$

10 🍴 Map p40, F5

Head here, inside the Grand Hôtel, for the famous smörgåsbord – especially during the Christmas holidays, when it becomes even more elaborate (reservations recommended). Arrive early for a window seat and tuck into both hot and cold Swedish staples, including gravadlax with almond potatoes, herring, meatballs and lingonberry jam. It's like a belt-busting crash course in classic Nordic flavours. (☑08-679 35 86; www.grandhotel.se; Södra Blasieholmshamnen 6, Grand Hôtel Stockholm; smörgåsbord 545kr, mains 205-365kr; ⏱7am-11pm, closed 10.30-11.30am; 🚇Kungsträdgården)

Holy Greens
VEGETARIAN $

9 🍴 Map p40, E4

This crisp, friendly cafe serves huge, healthful bowls of greens, grains and superfoods at good prices – try the Laxokado, with baked salmon, black rice, avocado, pickled veggies, sunflower seeds and greens, or the falafel bowl with a creamy lemon sauce, baby tomatoes and snap peas. Everything is available gluten-free. Add a shot of grapefruit-beet juice (20kr) for extra

virtue. (☑08-22 62 22; www.regeringsgatan.holygreens.se; Regeringsgatan 28; mains 85-105kr; ⏱8am-7pm Mon-Fri, 11am-5pm Sat & Sun; 🍴; 🚇T-Centralen)

Wiener Caféet
CAFE $$

10 🍴 Map p40, F3

Step into the lavish art-deco interior here and you are transported to the grand cafes of Vienna and Paris. Pastry chef Per Bäckström has ensured that this is the place to come in town for tea (2pm-5pm). And not just a cuppa, but a lavish Ritz Hotel-style experience including scones and cream, choux puffs and assorted cakes. (☑08-68 42 38 50; www.wienercafeet.com; Biblioteksgatan 6-8; mains 185-269kr, sandwiches 85-95kr, afternoon tea 329kr; ⏱7am-9pm Mon-Fri, 9.30am-9pm Sat, 9.30am-7pm Sun; 🛜; 🚌291, 🚇Östermalmstorg)

Operakällaren
FRENCH, SWEDISH $$$

11 🍴 Map p40, E5

Inside Stockholm's show-off opera house, the century-old Operakällaren is a major gastronomic event. Decadent chandeliers, golden mirrors and exquisitely carved ceilings set the scene for French-meets-fusion adventures like seared scallops with caramel, cauliflower purée, *pata negra* ham and brown-butter emulsion. Book at least two weeks ahead. (☑08-676 58 00; www.operakallaren.se; Karl XII's Torg 10; tasting menus 1050-5950kr; ⏱6pm-1am Tue-Sat, closed mid-Jul–mid-Aug; 🚇Kungsträdgården)

Local Life
Style City

Stockholm is a ludicrously fashionable city. Casual dress is OK for daytime, but you'll be conspicuous at nightclubs or top-end restaurants if you don't snazz it up. From September to May, bring a hat, gloves and scarf for nights out. Many clubs enforce a coat-check in winter; be prepared to hand over your top layer.

Drinking

Berns Salonger

BAR

12 Map p40, F4

A Stockholm institution since 1862, this glitzy entertainment palace remains one of the city's hottest party spots. While the gorgeous ballroom hosts some brilliant live-music gigs, the best of Berns' bars is in the intimate basement, packed with cool creative types, top-notch DJs and projected art-house images. Check the website for a schedule of events; some require advance ticket purchase. (📞08-56 63 22 00; www.berns.se; Berzelii Park; ⊙club 11pm-4am Thu-Sat, occasionally Wed & Sun, bar from 5pm daily; ⓇKungsträdgården)

Café Opera

CLUB

13 Map p40, E5

Rock stars need a suitably excessive place to schmooze, booze and groove, one with glittering chandeliers, ceiling frescoes and a jet-set vibe.

This bar-club combo fits the bill, but it's also welcoming enough to make regular folk *feel* like rock stars. If you only have time to hit one primo club during your visit, this is a good choice. (📞08-676 58 07; www.cafeopera.se; Karl XII's Torg; cover from 160kr; ⊙10pm-3am Wed-Sun; ⓇKungsträdgården)

East

BAR

14 Map p40, F2

East is a bar, restaurant and club rolled into one. Great cocktails make it a bartender hang-out. Dishes have a predominantly modern Asian twist (locals recommend the sushi), carrying influences from Vietnam, Korea and Japan. Set right in the heart of Östermalm on Stureplan, it's a good place for fuelling up before or during a club night. (📞08-611 49 59; http://east.se; Stureplan 13; dinner mains 247-385kr; ⊙11.30am-3am Mon-Sat, 5pm-3am Sun; ⓇÖstermalmstorg)

Solidaritet

CLUB

15 Map p40, F2

Solidaritet plays host to both Swedish and internationally renowned DJs with an emphasis on electronic music. The interior decor, designed by leading Swedish architects, is sleek and stylish. The club is set just off Stureplan, the centre of Stockholm's club and party scene. (📞08-678 10 50; www.solidaritet.eu; Lästmakargatan 3; ⊙11pm-5am Wed-Sat; ⓇÖstermalmstorg)

Understand

Swedish Film & TV

Sweden led the way in the silent-film era with such masterpieces as *Körkarlen (The Phantom Carriage)*. In 1967 came Vilgot Sjöman's notorious *I Am Curious – Yellow*, a subtly hilarious sociopolitical film that got more attention outside Sweden for its X rating than its sharp commentary.

Bergman

One man has largely defined modern Swedish cinema to the outside world: Ingmar Bergman. With deeply contemplative films such as *The Seventh Seal, Through a Glass Darkly* and *Persona*, the beret-topped director explored human alienation, the absence of God, the meaning of life, the certainty of death and other light-hearted themes.

Newer Names

More recently, the Swedish towns of Trollhättan and Ystad have become filmmaking centres, the former drawing the likes of director Lukas Moodysson, whose *Lilja 4-Ever, Show Me Love* and *Tillsammans* were popular and critical hits. Moodysson's newest film, 2014's *We Are the Best!*, is an uplifting movie about three high-schoolgirls in 1980s Stockholm who form a punk band out of spite.

Dragon Tattoo

The film version of Stieg Larsson's runaway hit novel, *The Girl with the Dragon Tattoo* (2009), stars Michael Nyqvist and Noomi Rapace and was a huge commercial success. The first instalment in Larsson's series was remade in English by director David Fincher, with Daniel Craig as journalist Mikael Blomkvist, mostly on location in Sweden.

TV

The Bridge, an excellent Danish–Swedish coproduction that has also had an American remake, is a bit grisly. But the unconventional police procedural reveals subtleties of Swedish life that are often overlooked: things like inter-Scandinavian tensions, sexual politics, treatment of minorities and immigrants, and not least, a particularly Scandinavian visual style.

Top Tip
Advance Tickets
Buy tickets in advance for acts you don't want to miss at Fasching or Glenn Miller Café. Same goes for opera, dance and theatre performances around Norrmalm – they do sell out.

Entertainment

Fasching
JAZZ

16 Map p40, B3

The pick of Stockholm's jazz clubs, Fasching has live music most nights. DJs often take over with Afrobeat, Latin, neo-soul or R&B on Friday night and retro-soul, disco and rare grooves on Saturday. (☑08-53 48 29 60; www.fasching.se; Kungsgatan 63; ◷6pm-1am Mon-Thu, to 4am Fri & Sat, 5pm-1am Sun; ᙁT-Centralen)

Operan
OPERA

17 Map p40, E5

This is the place to go for thunderous tenors, sparkling sopranos and classical ballet. It has some bargain tickets in seats with poor views, and occasional lunchtime concerts for 275kr. (☑08-791 44 00; www.operan.se; Gustav Adolfs Torg, Operahuset; tickets 240-1070kr; ᙁKungsträdgården)

Stockholms Stadsteatern
THEATRE

18 Map p40, D4

Regular performances are staged at this theatre inside Kulturhuset, as well as guest appearances by foreign theatre companies. It's also the temporary home to some of the collections from the National Gallery, which is closed for renovations. (☑08-50 62 02 00; www.stadsteatern.stockholm.se; Kulturhuset, Sergels Torg; tickets 200-350kr; ᙁT-Centralen)

Glenn Miller Café
JAZZ, BLUES

19 Map p40, D2

Simply loaded with character, this tiny jazz-and-blues bar draws a faithful, fun-loving crowd. It also serves excellent, affordable French-style classics like mussels with white wine sauce. Live music Wednesday to Saturday. (☑08-10 03 22; Brunnsgatan 21A; ◷5pm-1am Mon-Thu, to 2am Fri & Sat; ᙁHötorget)

Dansens Hus
DANCE

20 Map p40, B2

This place is an absolute must for contemporary-dance fans. Guest artists have included everyone from British choreographer Akram Khan to Canadian innovator Daniel Léveillé. (☑08-50 89 90 90; www.dansenshus.se; Barnhusgatan 12-14; tickets around 300kr, under 20yr half-price; ᙁT-Centralen)

Konserthuset
CLASSICAL MUSIC

21 Map p40, C2

Head to this pretty blue building for classical concerts and other musical marvels, including the Royal Philharmonic Orchestra. The bronze sculpture of nymphs frolicking out front (*Orpheus Well*) is by Carl Milles.

(📞08-50 66 77 88; www.konserthuset.se;
Hötorget; tickets 85-325kr; 🚇Hötorget)

Shopping

NK
DEPARTMENT STORE

22 🔒 Map p40, E3

An ultraclassy department store
founded in 1902, NK (Nordiska Kom-
paniet) is a city landmark – you can
see its rotating neon sign from most
parts of Stockholm. You'll find top-
name brands and several nice cafes,
and the basement levels are great for
stocking up on souvenirs and gourmet
groceries. Around Christmas, check
out its inventive window displays.
(📞08-762 80 00; www.nk.se; Hamngatan
12-18; ⏰10am-8pm Mon-Fri, 10am-6pm Sat,
11am-5pm Sun; 🚇T-Centralen)

Åhléns
DEPARTMENT STORE

23 🔒 Map p40, C3

For your all-in-one retail therapy,
scour department-store giant Åhléns.
It's especially good for housewares,
bedding and Swedish-made items to
bring home as gifts. (📞08-676 60 00;
Klarabergsgatan 50; ⏰10am-9pm Mon-Fri,
10am-7pm Sat, 11am-7pm Sun; 🚇T-Centralen)

PK Huset
SHOPPING CENTRE

24 🔒 Map p40, E3

One of the main shopping centres in
Stockholm's central shopping district.

Home to Swedish fashion brands and
Swedish staples such as Systembolaget
and Apotek. Next door to NK department store. (📞0768-71 50 10; www.pkhuset.
com; cnr Hamngatan & Norrlandsgatan;
⏰10am-8pm Mon-Fri, to 6pm Sat, to 5pm Sun;
🚇T-Centralen)

Mood Stockholm
MALL

25 🔒 Map p40, E3

Not quite shopping mall, not quite
galleria, Mood Stockholm oozes cool.
Straddling the shopping districts
of Östermalm and Norrmalm, it's
centrally located and a perfect escape
from the busy streets – ideal for a
shop, drink or meal with friends.
Home to both Swedish and internationally renowned brands. (📞08-696 31
00; http://moodstockholm.se; Regeringsgatan
48; ⏰10am-8pm Mon-Fri, to 6pm Sat, 11am-
5pm Sun; 🚇Hötorget, Östermalmstorg)

Gallerian
MALL

26 🔒 Map p40, D3

Stockholm's first shopping mall,
Gallerian is right in the middle of the
city's shopping districts. It hosts some
of Sweden's best-known brands as well
as international favourites. A great
opportunity to update your wardrobe
with some Swedish style or a central
point to take a break. (📞08-53 33 73 00;
Hamngatan 37; ⏰10am-8pm Mon-Fri, to 6pm
Sat, 11am to 6pm Sun; 🚇T-Centralen)

Explore

Djurgården & Skeppsholmen

The parklike island of Djurgården (pictured above) is a museum-goer's dream. Not only are many of Stockholm's top museums gathered here but the setting is sublime: gardens, greenery, a lazy river, cycle paths, picnic places, and all of it just one footbridge (or short summer ferry ride) away from the centre of town.

The Sights in a Day

☀ Get to **Skansen** (p52) early, and have a rough plan about which parts of it you most want to see – you'll probably need to pick and choose (you could easily spend a whole day here). Grab a snack where you make your exit, or stop for a post-Skansen lunch at **Wärdshuset Ulla Winbladh** (p67).

☀ Spend the next hour or two in one of the city's best-loved museums, **Vasamuseet** (p56), dedicated to the sunken battleship. If you're travelling as a family, another option is to send the kids to Vasamuseet while the parents check out the excellent **Spritmuseum** (p63), all about the history of booze and vice in Sweden. There's a great cafe there, as well.

☾ If you've planned cleverly, this is a Tuesday or a Friday, which means **Moderna Museet** (p58) is open until 8pm so you can take a leisurely stroll over to it and have plenty of time to look around. Wrap it up with a good meal at the museum's award-winning restaurant.

For a local's day in Djurgården, see p60.

◉ Top Sights

Skansen (p52)

Vasamuseet (p56)

Moderna Museet (p58)

◯ Local Life

Escape to Djurgården (p60)

♥ Best of Stockholm

Eating
Rosendals Trädgårdskafe (p66)

Museums & Galleries
Nordiska Museet (p63)

Spritmuseum (p63)

Prins Eugens Waldemarsudde (p61)

With Kids
Junibacken (p65)

Gröna Lund Tivoli (p66)

Aquaria Vattenmuseum (p64)

Getting There

🚍 **Bus** 44, 65, 69

🚋 **Tram** 7 from Norrmalmstorg

⛴ **Ferry** Djurgårdsfärjan Ferry services connect Djurgården to Slussen and Skeppsholmen every 10 minutes; SL passes are valid

Ⓜ **Metro** (Tunnelbana) Kungsträdgården, T-Centralen

Top Sights
Skansen

The world's first open-air museum, Skansen is a highlight of the city, one of a few attractions most locals will recommend. It occupies a large parklike area on a hillside, and traces the history of Swedish life through various traditional buildings, huts and houses. There's also a zoo of native animals, and a number of places to stop for refreshments.

👁 Map p62, C3

www.skansen.se

Djurgårdsvägen

adult/child 180/60kr

🕙 10am-6pm, extended hours in summer; Ⓟ

🚌 69, ⛴ Djurgårdsfärjan, 🚊 7

Nordic Zoo

The Skansen Zoo, with moose, reindeer, wolverines, lynx and other native wildlife, is a highlight, especially in spring when baby critters scamper around – the brown bear cubs are irresistible. Around 75 species of Scandinavian animals live in the zoo, along with a few imported species. There's also a petting zoo where young children can meet small animals.

Glassblowers' Workshop

The glassblowers' workshop is a popular stop: watching the intricate forms emerge from glowing blobs of liquid glass is transfixing. The shop was moved here from a Slussen basement in 1936 – the craftswoman in charge today is the third generation of the original family. If you're wondering, the temperature of the oven is 1130°C (2066°F).

Rescued Buildings

Within Skansen, there's a still-working bakery, a bank and post office, a machine shop, botanical gardens and Hazelius' mansion. Part of the pharmacy was moved here from Drottningholm castle; two little garden huts came from Tantolunden, a community garden still operating in Södermalm. There's also a Sami camp, farmsteads representing several regions, a manor house and a school.

Music & Events

Daily activities take place on Skansen's stages, including folk dancing and an enormous public festival at Midsummer's Eve (first Friday after 19 June). If you're in Stockholm for any of the country's major celebrations, such as Walpurgis Night (30 April) or St Lucia Day (13 December), it's a popular place to watch Swedes celebrate. In

☑ Top Tips

▶ Prices and hours vary seasonally and closing times for each workshop can vary. Check times online.

▶ From mid-June through August, Waxholmsbolaget ferries (www.waxholmsbolaget. se) run from Slussen to Djurgården; the route is part of the regular SL transit system, so you can use your SL pass to board. It's about a five-minute trip and runs every 10 minutes or so.

▶ A map and an excellent booklet in English are available.

▶ You can take the escalator to the top of the park and make your way downhill.

✗ Take a Break

Skansen has a number of cafes, restaurants, hot-dog and ice-cream stands on-site. Stop in at the traditional bakery for a coffee and pastry or lunch.

Understand
Living History

Buildings in the open-air museum represent various trades and areas of industry from Sweden's earliest days. In most of them you'll find staff dressed up in period costume, often making crafts, playing music or churning butter while cheerfully answering questions about the folk whose lives they're recreating. It's potentially a bit silly, but endearing in this setting.

summer, check out Allsång, a televised singalong on Skansen's main stage.

Aquarium

The **Skansen Akvariet** (☎08-442 80 39; www.skansen.se; adult/child 100/60kr; ⏰10am-4pm or 5pm, closing times vary by season; 🚌7) is worth a wander, with residents such as piranhas, lemurs and pygmy marmosets (the smallest monkeys in the world). Intrepid visitors may be allowed into the cages of some of the animals – check the daily schedule posted at Skansen's main gate. (Unlike most museums inside Skansen, the aquarium has a separate admission fee.

Vastveit Storehouse

There's a top-heavy little wooden hut at the far northern side of Skansen – called Vastveit, it's a storehouse that was imported from Norway and is reportedly the oldest building in the park, with parts dating from the 14th century. The shape is typical of traditional Swedish mountain and farmstead huts; many are still in use.

Dalahäst

Look for the giant wooden horse, or Dalahäst, a favourite photo op for smaller kids. You'll find it and other playground equipment on Orsakullen, an open area right in the centre of Skansen, which is also conveniently near some restrooms and snack kiosks. Souvenir wooden horses in more portable sizes can be found in the main Skansen gift shop (and all over town).

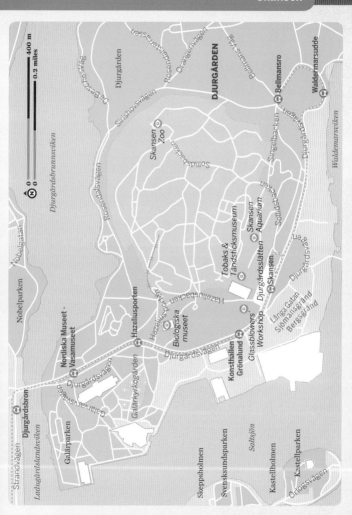

Top Sights
Vasamuseet

A good-humoured glorification of some dodgy calculations, Vasamuseet is the custom-built home of the massive warship *Vasa*. The ship, a whopping 69m long and 48.8m tall, was the pride of the Swedish crown when it set off on its maiden voyage on 10 August 1628. Within minutes, the top-heavy vessel tipped and sank to the bottom of Saltsjön, along with many of the people on board. The museum details its painstaking retrieval and restoration, as well as putting the whole thing into historical context.

👁 Map p62, B2

www.vasamuseet.se

Galärvarvsvägen 14

adult/child 130kr/free

🕐8.30am-6pm Jun-Aug, 10am-5pm Sep-May; Ⓟ

🚌44, ⛴Djurgårdsfärjan, 🚋7

Artefacts from the *Vasa*

Exhibits

Five levels of exhibits cover artefacts salvaged from the *Vasa,* life on board, naval warfare and 17th-century sailing and navigation, plus sculptures and temporary exhibitions. The bottom-floor exhibition is particularly fascinating, using modern forensic science to recreate the faces and life stories of several of the ill-fated passengers. The ship was painstakingly raised in 1961 and reassembled like a giant 14,000-piece jigsaw. Almost all of what you see today is original.

Meanwhile

Putting the catastrophic fate of the *Vasa* in historical context is a permanent multimedia exhibit, *Meanwhile*. With images of events and moments happening simultaneously around the globe – from China to France to 'New Amsterdam', from traders and settlers to royal families to working mothers and put-upon merchants – it establishes a vivid setting for the story at hand.

Scale Model

On the entrance level is a model of the ship at scale 1:10, painted according to a thoroughly researched understanding of how the original would've looked. Once you've studied it, look for the intricately carved decorations adorning the actual *Vasa*. The stern in particular is gorgeous – it was badly damaged but has been slowly and carefully restored.

Upper Deck

A reconstruction of the upper gun deck allows visitors to get a feel for what it might have been like to be on a vessel this size. The *Vasa* had two gun decks, which held an atypically large number of cannons – thought to be part of the reason it capsized.

☑ **Top Tips**

▶ Guided tours in English depart from the front entrance every 30 minutes in summer.

▶ Near the entrance of the museum is a cinema screening a 25-minute film covering topics not included in the exhibitions.

▶ You can climb aboard the reconstructed upper gun deck, but the actual ship is off-limits for its safety.

✕ **Take a Break**

There's a restaurant inside the museum, serving coffee, drinks and full meals. Outside the museum, you're not far from Wärdshuset Ulla Winbladh (p67), which also has inviting outdoor seating areas.

Top Sights
Moderna Museet

Moderna Museet is Stockholm's modern-art maverick, with a fabulous permanent collection of paintings, sculpture, photography, video art and installations. Highlights include works by Pablo Picasso, Salvador Dalí, Andy Warhol and Damien Hirst, as well as their Scandinavian contemporaries and plenty of not-yet-household names. The museum also stages a number of temporary exhibits and career retrospectives each year (usually with a separate admission fee), often focused on Scandinavian artists.

Map p62, A2

08-52 02 35 00

www.modernamuseet.se

Exercisplan 4; admission free

10am-8pm Tue & Fri, to 6pm Wed-Thu, 11am-6pm Sat & Sun; P

65, Djurgårdsfärjan

1900s to 1940s

The galleries on the museum's main floor are arranged roughly by era, although things do tend to move around (and a large section is used for temporary exhibitions, usually with a separate admission fee). In the first of the permanent collection's three sections, you're likely to find early modernists like Edvard Munch and Ernst Ludwig Kirchner, Georgio de Chirico and several pieces by Marcel Duchamp.

Postwar to 1970s

Continuing through the main floor, you'll reach what are likely the most familiar names: Francis Bacon, Salvador Dalí, Robert Rauschenberg, Georges Braque and Pablo Picasso, plus an enormous and exuberant Henri Matisse cut-out covering one whole wall.

1970s to the Present

The farthest section usually holds the newest additions to the permanent collection, and as such is the most frequently changing. Things you might find here include Barbara Kruger paintings, Donald Judd installations, and envelope-pushing work by artists most of us haven't heard of yet, alongside important work by well-established Scandinavian artists.

Outdoor Sculptures

Arranged on the grounds around the museum are several sculptures by a wide variety of artists. The most attention-grabbing are the large colourful figures by Niki di Saint Phalle and Jean Tinguely, called *The Fantastic Paradise*. There's also an Alexander Calder and a Picasso, and work by several Swedish sculptors in the walled sculpture garden.

GELIA/GETTY IMAGES ©

☑ **Top Tips**

▶ Remember that the museum is closed on Mondays.

▶ Keep in mind that the permanent collection is rearranged frequently, and items from the collection are sometimes loaned out to other museums.

✕ **Take a Break**

There's a fabulous and very popular restaurant inside the museum with a great view over the water; an espresso bar in the foyer (next to the dreamy bookstore); and the small, casual **Cafe Blom**, a great place for lunch in a nice secluded courtyard.

Local Life
Escape to Djurgården

In a perfect world, every city would have a place like Djurgården, a quiet, leafy green retreat from the noise and traffic of the working world. It is literally steps away from the heart of downtown Stockholm, but the park island feels like an otherworldly oasis. Part is occupied by Skansen and other excellent museums, but most consists of quiet trails through fields and forests, where locals exercise, picnic or just wander around.

1 Blue Gate

As soon as you walk across the bridge (Djurgårdsbron) from Norrmalm to Djurgården, you'll see a huge, bright-blue wrought-iron gate to your left. Go ahead and walk through it, and you'll be on the footpath alongside Djurgårdsbrunnsviken, the long stretch of water that separates Djurgården from Ladugårdsgärdet to the north. Stay on the trail along the water's edge,

stopping to admire baby ducks and passing boats as they appear.

❷ Rosendal

Eventually you'll reach signs pointing you towards **Rosendals Slott** (📞08-402 61 30; www.kungahuset.se; Rosendalsvägen 49; adult/child 100/50kr; ⏱hourly tours noon-3pm Tue-Sun Jun-Aug; 🚌44, 69, 🚋7). Rosendal was built as a palace for Karl XIV Johan in the 1820s. One of Sweden's finest examples of the Empire style, it sparkles with sumptuous royal furnishings. Admission is by guided tour only – but even just the setting is well worth going to, and it's a handy landmark to orient yourself on the island.

❸ Botanical Gardens

The *trädgård* or botanical gardens attached to Rosendals Slott are well worth a look. They're designed as a forum for educating the public on the techniques and possibilities of organic gardening, but they're also just fun to wander through. You'll see everything from herbs and roses to vegetables and wine grapes – and of course an organic compost heap. King Oscar I built the orangery in 1848.

❹ Biskopsudden

This area sticks out a bit from the main island, which means it has excellent views across the water at the surrounding parts of Stockholm. There's

a little cafe by the marina, **Cafe Ekorren** (www.cafeekorren.se; Biskopsvägen 5; mains 185-225kr; ⏱10am-8pm May-Sep; 🚌47, 69), with outdoor tables beside the water as well as a little yellow hut for indoor seating. It's a great place to kick your feet up for a while and have a coffee or an ice cream. (Full meals are also available.)

❺ Waldemarsudde Garden Trails

The grounds around the highly recommended **Prins Eugens Waldemarsudde** (Map p62, E4; 📞08-54 58 37 07; www.waldemarsudde.com; Prins Eugens väg 6; adult/child 150kr/free; ⏱11am-5pm Tue-Sun, to 8pm Thu, gardens 8am-9pm; 🚋7) gallery are equally well worth a visit – they're beautifully arranged, with multiple levels of walking paths and unexpected waterside gazebos that provide any number of picturesque views from different vantage points. Prins Eugen's grave is here, in a small, peaceful copse. Bring your camera and explore.

❻ Estonia Monument

As you wander back towards the bridge where the walk began, you'll pass the busy museums around Skansen. Take a small detour to visit the Estonia Monument. The structure was built to commemorate the ferry disaster of 28 September 1994, in which 852 people drowned when a boat en route from Tallinn capsized in stormy weather.

200 m
0.1 miles

Tekniska 4 ◉
Museet

De Besches Väg

Rosendalsterrassen

14 ⊗

Thielska 3 ◉ ▷
Galleriet

Valmundsvägen

Djurgårdsvägen

Prins Eugens Väg

Djurgården

Rosendalsvägen

Sirishovsvägen

Orangerivägen

DJURGÅRDEN

Bellmansro

Prins Eugens
Waldemarsudde
10 ◉

Dag Hammarskjölds väg

Nobelgatan

Djurgårdsbrunnsviken

Skansen

Solfjäderbacken

Singelbacken

Djurgårdsvägen

Waldemarsudde

Waldemarsviken

Ulrikagatan

Hazellusporten

16 ⊗

Hazellusporten

Tram Line 7

Tobaks & 12 ◉ Tändstickmuseum
Grönalund
Skansen ◉ 13
Konsthallen 15 ⊗ Skansen ⊞
Aquaria 6 ◉ 5 ◉ Djurgårdsslätten
Vattenmuseum Lund Tivoli
Gröna
ABBA: The Museum Gröna
Lila Allmänna Lund
Gränd

Beckholmen

Narvavägen

Sjöcaféet 9 ◉
Djurgårdsbron
Visit Djurgården ⓘ
Junibacken ◉ 8
Galärvarvsvägen

Nordiska
Museet –
Vasamuseet
Nordiska Museet
Galärvarvsgården ◉ 1
Spritmuseum
2 ◉

Vasamuseet ◉

Strandvägen

Riddargatan

Styrmansgatan

Grevgatan

Gärdet

Ladugårdslandsviken

Tyghusparken

Galärparken

Stockström Kanalbolaget
Svensksundsparken

Slupskjulsvägen
Arkitektur- och
Designcentrum
Moderna ◉
Museet
Batteriparken
Exercisplan 11 ◉
Långa Raden

Skeppsholmen

Saltsjön

Kastellholmen

Kastellparken

Amiralitetsparken

Strömmen

For reviews see	
◉ Top Sights	p52
◉ Sights	p63
⊗ Eating	p66

Nordiska Museet

Sights

Nordiska Museet
MUSEUM

 Map p62, B2

The epic Nordiska Museet is Sweden's largest cultural-history museum and one of its largest indoor spaces. The building itself (from 1907) is an eclectic, Renaissance-style castle designed by Isak Gustav Clason, who also drew up Östermalms Saluhall (p90); you'll notice a resemblance. Inside is a sprawling collection of all things Swedish, from sacred Sami objects to clothing and table settings. The museum boasts the world's largest collection of paintings by August Strindberg, as well as a number of his personal possessions.

(☎ 08-51 95 47 70; www.nordiskamuseet.se; Djurgårdsvägen 6-16; adult/child 120kr/free; ⊙ 10am-5pm Sep-May, 9am-5pm rest of year, to 8pm Wed; 🚌 44, 69, 🚢 Djurgårdsfärjan, 🚋 7)

Spritmuseum
MUSEUM

2 Map p62, B2

The surprisingly entertaining Museum of Spirits is dedicated to Sweden's complicated relationship with alcohol, as mediated over the years by the state-run monopoly System Bolaget. The slick space, in two 18th-century naval buildings, covers the history, manufacture and consumption of all kinds of booze, plus holiday traditions, drinking songs, food pairings and so on. Best of all, you can combine your

Top Tip

Forward Planning

For the big-ticket museums (ABBA, for example), it's best to buy tickets online, reserving a visiting time in advance.

visit with a tasting kit (250kr), including various flavours of liquor to be sampled at specified points. (Museum of Spirits; ☑08-12 13 13 00; www.spritmuseum.se; Djurgårdsvägen 38; adult/child 120kr/free; ⊙10am-5pm Mon, to 7pm Tue-Sat, noon-5pm Sun; ⬚44, 69, ⛴Djurgårdsfärjan, ⬚7)

Thielska Galleriet
GALLERY

 3 ◉ Map p62, E3

Thielska Galleriet, at the far eastern end of Djurgården, is a must for Nordic art fans, with a savvy collection of late-19th- and early-20th-century works from Scandinavian greats like Carl Larsson, Anders Zorn, Ernst Josephson and Bruno Liljefors, plus a series of Edvard Munch's etchings of vampiric women and several paintings from a bridge you'll recognise from *The Scream.* (Ernest Thiel, a banker and translator, was one of Munch's patrons.) (☑08-662 58 84; www.thielska-galleriet.se; Sjötullsbacken 8; adult/child 130kr/free; ⊙noon-5pm Tue-Sun, to 8pm Thu; ⬚69)

Tekniska Museet
MUSEUM

4 ◉ Map p62, E1

Tekniska is a sprawling wonderland of interactive science and technology

exhibits. The Teknorama is a vast room of kinetic experiments and stations designed to do things like test your balance, flexibility and strength. In one corner is a dark and genuinely scary mining exhibit. There's also a model railroad, a survey of inventions by women, and a climate-change game. (Museum of Science & Technology; ☑08-450 56 00; www.teknikamuseet.se; Museivägen 7; adult/child 150/100kr, free 5-8pm Wed; ⊙10am-5pm Thu-Tue, to 8pm Wed; ♿; ⬚69 Museiparken)

ABBA: The Museum
MUSEUM

5 ◉ Map p62, C3

A sensory-overload experience that might appeal only to devoted ABBA fans, this long-awaited and wildly hyped cathedral to the demigods of Swedish pop is almost aggressively entertaining. It's packed to the gills with memorabilia and interactivity – every square inch has something new to look at, be it a glittering guitar, a vintage photo of Benny, Björn, Frida or Agnetha, a classic music video, an outlandish costume or a tour van from the band members' early days. (☑08-12 13 28 60; www.abbathemuseum.com; Djurgårdsvägen 68; adult/child 250/95kr; ⊙9am-7pm Mon-Fri Jun-Aug, shorter hours rest of year; ⬚67, ⛴Djurgårdsfärjan, Emelie, ⬚7)

Aquaria Vattenmuseum
MUSEUM

6 ◉ Map p62, B3

This conservation-themed aquarium, complete with seahorses, sharks, piranhas and clownfish, takes you through various environmental zones – from tropical jungle and coral reef to sewer systems – with an emphasis on ecology and the fragility of the marine environment. If that sounds a bit of a drag, it's not – there's enough to do and see to keep the family entertained. Time your visit to coincide with a feeding, daily at 11am, 1.30pm and 2.30pm. (☎08-660 90 89; www.aquaria.se; Falkenbergsgatan 2; adult/child 120/80kr; ☉10am-6pm Jun-Aug, 10am-4.30pm Tue-Sun rest of year; 👪; ☒44, 69, ⛴Djurgårdsfärjan, ☒7)

Strömma Kanalbolaget BOATING

7 ◎ Map p62, A3

This ubiquitous company offers tours large and small, from a 50-minute 'royal canal tour' around Djurgården (200kr) to a 50-minute ABBA tour, which visits places where the *ABBA* movie was shot and drops you off at the ABBA museum (315kr). There are also hop-on, hop-off tours by bus (from 300kr), boat (180kr) or both (400kr). (☎08-12 00 40 00; www.stromma.se; Svensksundsvägen 17; 220-400kr)

Junibacken AMUSEMENT PARK

8 ◎ Map p62, B2

Junibacken whimsically recreates the fantasy scenes of Astrid Lindgren's books for children. Catch the flying Story Train over Stockholm, shrink to the size of a sugar cube and end up at Villekulla cottage, where kids can shout, squeal and dress up like Pippi Longstocking. The bookshop is

a treasure trove of children's books, as well as a great place to pick up anything from cheeky Karlsson dolls to cute little art cards with storybook themes. (www.junibacken.se; Djurgården; adult/child 159/139kr; ☉10am-6pm Jul-Aug, to 5pm rest of year; 👪; ☒44, 69, ⛴Djurgårdsfärjan, ☒7)

Sjöcaféet CYCLING

9 ◎ Map p62, B1

Rent bicycles from the small wooden hut below this restaurant, cafe and tourist-info centre beside Djurgårdsbron; they also offer canoes and kayaks for hire. (☎08-660 57 57; www.sjocafeet.se; Djurgårdsvägen 2; per hr/day bicycles 80/275kr, canoes 150/400kr, kayaks 125/400kr; ☉9am-9pm Apr-Sep; ☒7)

Prins Eugens Waldemarsudde MUSEUM

10 ◎ Map p62, E4

Prins Eugens Waldemarsudde, at the southern tip of Djurgården, is a soul-perking combo of water views and art. The palace once belonged to the painter prince (1865–1947), who favoured art over typical royal pleasures. In addition to Eugen's own work, it holds his impressive collection of Nordic paintings and sculptures, including works by Anders Zorn and Carl Larsson. The museum stages top-notch temporary exhibitions several times a year, usually highlighting the careers of important Scandinavian artists. (☎08-54 58 37 07; www.waldemarsudde.com; Prins Eugens väg

Local Life
On the Island
Jogging Stockholmers make excellent use of the running trails that lace Djurgården. Alternatively (you're on holiday, after all), this whole island is a picnicker's dream; bring a towel or blanket, a novel and a swimsuit to lounge away a sunny afternoon.

6; adult/child 150kr/free; ⏱11am-5pm Tue-Sun, to 8pm Thu, gardens 8am-9pm; 🚌7)

ArkDes   MUSEUM

11 ◉ Map p62, A3

Adjoining Moderna Museet (p58) and housed in a converted navy drill hall, the architecture and design centre has a permanent exhibition spanning 1000 years of Swedish architecture and an archive of 2.5 million documents, photographs, plans, drawings and models. Temporary exhibitions also cover international names and work. The museum organises occasional themed architectural tours of Stockholm; check the website or ask at the information desk. (📞08-58 72 70 00; www.arkdes.se; Exercisplan 4; special exhibits adult/child 120kr/free; ⏱10am-8pm Tue & Fri, to 6pm Wed & Thu, 11am-6pm Sat & Sun; 🚌65, 🚢Djurgårdsfärjan)

Tobaks &
Tändsticksmuseum   MUSEUM

12 ◉ Map p62, C3

Inside the vast open-air park of Skansen (p52), the Tobaks &

Tändsticksmuseum traces the history and culture of smoking and the manufacture of those iconic Swedish matches. (Tobacco & Matchstick Museum; 📞08-442 80 26; www.tobaksochtandsticks museum.se; admission free; ⏱11am-5pm, closed Mon Oct-Apr; 🚌7)

Gröna Lund Tivoli   AMUSEMENT PARK

13 ◉ Map p62, C3

Crowded Gröna Lund Tivoli has some 30 rides, ranging from the tame (a German circus carousel) to the terrifying (the Free Fall, where you drop from a height of 80m in six seconds). There are countless places to eat and drink in the park, but whether you'll keep anything down is another matter entirely. The Åkband day pass gives unlimited rides, or individual rides range from 25kr to 75kr. (www.gronalund. com; Lilla Allmänna Gränd 9; entrance 115kr, unlimited ride pass 330kr; ⏱10am-11pm Jun-Aug, shorter hours rest of year; 🚻; 🚌44, 🚢Djurgårdsfärjan, 🚌7)

Eating

Rosendals
Trädgårdskafe   CAFE $$

14 ✕ Map p62, E2

Set among the greenhouses of a pretty botanical garden, Rosendals is an idyllic spot for heavenly pastries and coffee or a meal and a glass of organic wine. Lunch includes a brief menu of soups, sandwiches and gorgeous salads. Much of the produce is biodynamic and grown on-site.

Gröna Lund Tivoli

(☎08-54 58 12 70; www.rosendalstradgard.
se; Rosendalsterrassen 12; mains 99-145kr;
⏰11am-5pm Mon-Fri, to 6pm Sat & Sun May-
Sep, closed Mon Feb-Apr & Oct-Dec; 🅿🕿;
🚌44, 69, 76 Djurgårdsbron, 🚋7)

Blå Porten Café
CAFE $$

15 🍴 Map p62, C3

This lovely cafe with a courtyard
garden is located in the shadow of
Liljevalchs Konsthall (☎08-50 83 13 30;
www.liljevalchs.se; Djurgårdsvägen 60; 🚌44,
69, ⛴Djurgårdsfärjan, 🚋7) – and, at the
time of our last visit, was more or less
demolished to enable repairs to the
art gallery. It's scheduled to reopen
in summer 2018. (☎08-663 87 59; www.
blaporten.com; Djurgårdsvägen 64; 🕿; 🚌47
Liljevalc Gröna Lund, 🚋7 Liljevalc Gröna Lund)

Wärdshuset
Ulla Winbladh
SWEDISH $$$

16 🍴 Map p62, C2

Named after one of Carl Michael
Bellman's lovers, this villa was built
as a steam bakery for the Stockholm
World's Fair (1897) and now serves
fine food in intimate rooms and a
blissful garden setting. Sup on skil-
fully prepared upscale versions of
traditional Scandi favourites, mostly
built around fish and potatoes – try
the herring plate with homemade
crispbread. (☎08-53 48 97 01; www.
ullawinbladh.se; Rosendalsvägen 8; mains
175-425kr; ⏰11.30am-10pm Mon, 11.30am-
11pm Tue-Fri, 12.30-11pm Sat, 12.30-10pm Sun;
⛴Djurgårdsfärjan, 🚋7)

Explore

Södermalm

Slightly unvarnished and bohemian, Stockholm's southern island is where you'll find the coolest secondhand shops, art galleries, bars and espresso labs. The hills at the island's northern edge provide stunning views across Gamla Stan and the rest of the central city. A couple of museum heavyweights round out the to-do list, before taking in some of the city's most diverse nightlife.

The Sights in a Day

☀ Though known for its nightlife, Södermalm is also home to the great **Fotografiska** museum (p70).

☀ After you've explored the photography museum, stop for some refreshments and perhaps a veggie lunch at **Chutney** (p76) – an excellent-value and very cosy little cafe. From here, a stroll along busy Götgatan and back along any of its parallel streets will give you a sense of the neighbourhood.

🌙 Make your way back towards Slussen around dusk, when it's ideal to climb the Söder cliffs and wander tiny Monteliusvägen – a footpath that provides awesome views over the city. By then, you've earned a beer: stroll over and choose from the vast selection of brews at **Akkurat** (p79).

For a local's night bar-hopping in Södermalm, see p72.

◉ **Top Sight**
Fotografiska (p70)

🔍 **Local Life**
Södermalm Bar-Hopping (p72)

💟 **Best of Stockholm**

Eating
Hermans Trädgårdscafé (p76)

Woodstockholm (p76)

Mahalo (p78)

Chutney (p76)

Pelikan (p77)

Nightlife
Akkurat (p79)

Kvarnen (p78)

Debaser Strand (p79)

Fashion
Judits (p81)

Lisa Larsson Second Hand (p80)

Smiley Vintage (p81)

Design
DesignTorget (p81)

Getting There

Ⓜ **Metro** (Tunnelbana) Slussen, Medborgarplatsen, Zinkensdamm

Top Sights
Fotografiska

A must for shutterbugs, the temporary exhibitions at this stylish photography museum are well curated and presented; examples have included a Robert Mapplethorpe retrospective and portraits by indie filmmaker Gus Van Sant. Fotografiska draws big crowds and offers photography courses, as well as staging occasional concerts and other one-off events. And it has one of the coolest locations in Stockholm.

👁 Map p74, G2

www.fotografiska.eu

Stadsgårdshamnen 22

adult/child 135kr/free

🕘9am-11pm Sun-Wed, to 1am Thu-Sat

🚉Slussen

Temporary Exhibitions

In addition to its permanent collection, the museum holds four major temporary exhibitions a year, often in the form of retrospectives of big-name artists, as well as 15 to 20 smaller temporary exhibits. Memorable shows have featured enormous photos by Sebastião Salgado, an Irving Penn retrospective, and an exhibit of work by the Young Nordic Photographer of the Year, Akseli Valmunen. Others have included the likes of Annie Leibovitz, David LaChapelle, Klara Kallstrom and Johan Wik.

Film & Video

Some of the museum's temporary exhibitions incorporate short films and video, displayed on loops in small rooms tucked into various corners. Be sure to seek these out – it's often some of the most provocative and fascinating work in the gallery.

The Building

Fotografiska is housed in a massive (5500 sq metre) industrial art-nouveau brick structure designed by the well-known architect Ferdinand Boberg and built in 1906. It was originally a customs hall, and underwent a 250kr million renovation to transform the interior for the museum before opening in 2010.

Gift Shop

Plan to spend some time browsing the gift shop, as it's particularly well stocked. The collection of eccentric little cameras alone is interesting, but there are also hundreds of photos available to purchase and, of course, photography books, postcards and posters.

☑ Top Tips

▶ The Slussen area is set to be a construction zone for the next several years, so follow signs carefully from the tunnelbana station to reach the museum.

▶ In the summer months, the terrace in front of the museum entrance becomes a lively bar and cafe serving cocktails and a brief menu of dinner specials and filling salads, usually with pumping DJ music in the background.

✗ Take a Break

The cafe on the museum's top floor serves coffee and cakes, decadent sandwiches and salads year-round, and the view from its panoramic windows is awesome.

Ready to leave the museum? Climb the stairs behind the building to Hermans Trädgårdscafé (p76) for a veggie buffet with a view.

Local Life
Bar-Hopping in Södermalm

It's a well-established fact that any neighbourhood where artists and bohemian types live and work is a good place for a bar hop. In Stockholm, Söder is that neighbourhood, and the bars range from comfy dives to beautifully designed jewel boxes. The unifying factor, even in the coolest bars, is an unfussy open-mindedness. This part of town is all about fun.

❶ Medborgarplatsen
At the edges of the vast open square that is Medborgarplatsen, all the bars in the area have roped-off outdoor seating. We recommend choosing a spot at whichever place offers the best eye candy.

❷ Mariatorget
Trek slightly northwest towards the lovely square Mariatorget, where you can enjoy a drink on the terrace or

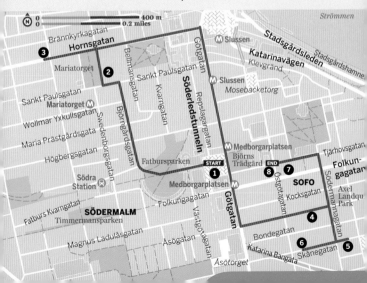

balcony of the ABBA-owned hotel **Rival** (📞08-54 57 89 24; www.rival.se; Mariatorget 3; ⏰5pm-midnight Thu-Sat; 🚇Mariatorget).

❸ Marie Laveau

In an old sausage factory along Hornsgatan, **Marie Laveau** (www.marielaveau.se; Hornsgatan 66; ⏰5-11pm Mon & Tue, to 3am Wed-Sat; 🚇Mariatorget) is a kicking Söder playpen that draws a boho-chic crowd. The designer-grunge bar (think chequered floor and subway-style tiled columns) serves killer cocktails, while the sweaty basement hosts club nights on the weekend. Known for its monthly 'Bangers & Mash' Britpop night – check online for a schedule.

❹ Nada

Loop back towards the action: SoFo, south of Folkungagatan. **Nada** (Map p74, F4; 📞08-644 70 20; Åsögatan 140; ⏰5pm-1am Mon-Sat; 🚇Medborgarplatsen) is a cosy establishment that pulls in a 20-/30-something crowd eager to party. DJs play an eclectic mix, from '80s retro to alternative pop, while behind the bar mixologists create sophisticated summery cocktails.

❺ Snotty's

Snotty's (Skånegatan 90; ⏰4pm-1am; 🚇Medborgarplatsen) is a mellow hangout a few blocks away from Nada. Friendly and free of attitude, this is one of the most comfortable and unpretentious places to drink in Stockholm. It has a vaguely retro vibe, a smooth wooden bar and record covers all over the walls.

❻ Bara Enkelt

Just down the street from Snotty's, decked out in shagalicious floral wallpaper and plush red sofas, **Bara Enkelt** (📞08-669 58 55; www.baras.se; Skånegatan 59; ⏰4pm-1am Mon-Fri, 3pm-1am Sat & Sun; 🚇Medborgarplatsen), formerly Bara Vi, is a popular hang-out for trendy 30-somethings who like their drinks list long and smooth. Check online for a schedule of indie rock acts on stage.

❼ Kebab Stop

Do as the locals do and stop for a greasy kebab at one of the carts on and around Medborgarplatsen – you'll need something to soak up all that adventure. For a sit-down version, try the friendly **Folkets Kebab** (📞08-669 91 66; Hornsgatan 92; buffet 119kr, kebabs from 50kr; ⏰10am-2am; 🚇Zinkensdamm).

❽ On the Corner

Wrap up the tour with a last stop at one of the very few places you can find a cheap beer in the city: the little collection of dive bars at the corner of Tjärhovsgatan and Östgötagatan. What they lack in ambience they make up for in affordability, and you're bound to meet a lively crowd here.

E   **F**   **G**   **H**

0   200 m
0   0.1 miles

Strömmen

Slussen

Sjöbergsplan

7 ⊗

Slussen Ⓜ

Södermalmstorg

Stadsgårdshamnen

Urvädersgränd

Katarinavägen

14 ⊗⊗15   Klevgränd

Ⓜ Slussen   2 ⊗

⊙ Fotografiska

Mosebacketorg

Stadsgårdshamnen

3 ⊗   **Stadsgårdsleden**

Fjällgatan

Master Mikaels Gata

Högbergsgatan

🔒 19

Stigbergsgatan

Lilla Erstagatan

Erstagatan

Medborgarplatsen   Kapellgränd

Björns Trädgård

Tjärhovsplan

Stigbergsparken

Medborgarplatsen

Tjärhovsgatan

🅿 9

Folkungagatan

Ⓜ Medborgarplatsen

SOFO

Nytorgsgatan

Renstiernas Gata

Borgmästargatan

Beckbrännarbacken

Åsögatan

Sagargatan

20 🔒

Axel Landquist Park

Kocksgatan

Östgötagatan

13 🅿   🔒 18   ⊗ 6

Klippgatan

Bondegatan

11 🅿

Söderledstunneln

Götgatan

Bondegatan

Skånegatan

⊗ 4

Nytorget

Katarina Bangata

Greta Garbos Torg

Tjurbergsgatan

Allhellgonagatan

Blekingegatan

⊗ 5

Ⓜ Skanstull

Gotlandsgatan

Bjurholmsplan

Ölandsgatan

Södermannagatan

Katarina Bangata

Malmgårdsvägen

Vita Bergen

Ringvägen

Lilla Blecktornsparken

Ljusterögatan

Sights

Tantolunden
PARK

1 Map p74, A3

Located in southwest Södermalm, adjacent to trendy Hornstull, Tantolunden is one of Stockholm's most extensive and varied parks. Its combination of allotments, open expanses, outdoor gym, play area and waterside walks make it a great getaway from the city centre. Although the park becomes a focal point of the city in the summer, with crowds flocking to swim and picnic, locals wind down with relaxing walks here throughout the year. (Zinkens Väg; 🚇 Zinkensdamm, Hornstull)

Eating

Woodstockholm
SWEDISH $$$

2 Map p74, E2

This hip dining spot incorporates a wine bar and furniture store showcasing chairs and tables by local designers. The menu changes weekly and is themed, somewhat wackily: think Salvador Dalí or Aphrodisiac, the latter including scallops with oyster

> ☑ Top Tip
> **Free Wi-fi**
> Right across Stockholm, wi-fi is almost always free and available at cafes, bus and train stations, hotels, hostels, 7-11 stores, ferries and on some trains.

mushrooms and sweetbreads with yellow beets and horseradish cream. This is fast becoming one of the city's classic foodie destinations. Reservations essential. (📞 08-36 93 99; www.woodstockholm.com; Mosebacketorg 9; mains 265-285kr; ⏱ 11.30am-2pm Mon, 11.30am-2pm & 5-11pm Tue-Sat; 🛜; 🚇 Slussen)

Hermans Trädgårdscafé
VEGETARIAN $$

3 Map p74, G2

This justifiably popular vegetarian buffet is one of the nicest places to dine in Stockholm, with a glassed-in porch and outdoor seating on a terrace overlooking the city's glittering skyline. Fill up on inventive, flavourful veggie and vegan creations served from a cosy, vaulted room – you might need to muscle your way in, but it's worth the effort. (📞 08-643 94 80; www.hermans.se; Fjällgatan 23B; buffet 195kr, desserts from 35kr; ⏱ 11am-9pm; 🖊; 🚌 2, 3, 53, 71, 76 Tjärhovsplan, 🚇 Slussen)

Chutney
VEGETARIAN $$

4 Map p74, F4

Sitting among a string of three inviting cafes along this block, Chutney is one of Stockholm's many well-established vegetarian restaurants, offering excellent value and great atmosphere. The daily lunch special is usually a deliciously spiced, Asian- or Indian-influenced mountain of veggies over rice, and includes salad, bread and coffee. (📞 08-640 30 10; www.chutney.se; Katarina Bangata 19; daily special weekday/weekend

Tantolunden

105/135kr; ⏰11am-10pm Mon-Fri, noon-10pm Sat, noon-9pm Sun; 🏃; 🚇Medborgarplatsen)

Pelikan

SWEDISH $$$

 5 Map p74, F5

Lofty ceilings, wood panelling and no-nonsense waiters in waistcoats set the scene for classic *husmanskost* (home cooking) at this century-old beer hall – think roasted reindeer, Västerbotten cheese pie and Arctic char. The herring options are particularly good (try the 'SOS' starter, an assortment of pickled herring (135kr to 195kr) and there's usu-ally a vegetarian special. There's a hefty list of aquavit, too. (☎08-55 60 90 90; www.pelikan.se; Blekingegatan 40; mains 188-335kr; ⏰5pm-midnight or 1am; 🚇Skanstull)

String

CAFE $

6 Map p74, G4

This retro-funky SoFo cafe does a bar-gain weekend brunch buffet (9am to 1pm Saturday and Sunday). Load your plate with everything from cereals, yoghurt and fresh fruit to pancakes. Its daily lunch specials are good value, too. (☎08-714 85 14; www.facebook.com/caf-estring; Nytorgsgatan 38; sandwiches 65-95kr; breakfast buffet 90kr; ⏰9am-10pm Mon-Thu, to 7pm Fri-Sun; 🚇Medborgarplatsen)

Nystekt Strömming

SWEDISH $

7 Map p74, E1

For a quick snack of freshly fried herring, seek out this humble cart

ROLF_52/GETTY IMAGES ©

Södra Teatern and Mosebacke Etablissement (p80)

outside the tunnelbana station at Slussen. Large or small combo plates come with big slabs of the fish and a selection of sides and condiments, from mashed potato and red onion to salads and hardbread; more-portable wraps and the delicious herring burger go for 55kr. (Södermalmstorg; mains 40-75kr; ⊙11am-9pm; 🚇Slussen)

Mahalo   VEGAN $$

8 🍴 Map p74, B2

You'll start to feel healthier just walking into this vegan cafe (formerly Hälsocafet), humming with plants and vivid colours. The focus is on huge, filling, eco-friendly superfood bowls, like the Buddha bowl (spicy tofu, greens, glass noodles, avocado) or the homemade-falafel and hummus bowl.

Coffee is included. There are also vegan sweets, wraps, breakfast bowls, smoothies, and turmeric or matcha lattes. (Hälsocafet; 🕿08-42 05 65 44; www.halsocafet.se; Hornsgatan 61; mains 85-139kr; ⊙9am-7pm Mon & Tue, 9am-8pm Wed-Fri, 10am-8pm Sat, 10am-7pm Sun; 🛜👣; 🚇Mariatorget, Zinkensdamm)

Drinking

Kvarnen   BAR

9 🍸 Map p74, E3

An old-school Hammarby football fan hang-out, Kvarnen is one of the best bars in Söder. The gorgeous beer hall dates from 1907 and seeps tradition; if you're not the clubbing type, get here early for a nice pint and a meal (mains from 210kr). As the night progresses, the nightclub vibe takes over. Queues are fairly constant but justifiable. (☎08-643 03 80; www.kvarnen. com; Tjärhovsgatan 4; ☺11am-1am Mon & Tue, to 3am Wed-Fri, noon-3am Sat, noon-1am Sun; 🚇Medborgarplatsen)

Akkurat
BAR

10 Map p74, D2

Valhalla for beer fiends, Akkurat boasts a huge selection of Belgian ales as well as a good range of Swedish-made microbrews and hard ciders. It's one of only two places in Sweden to be recognised by a Cask Marque for its real ale. Extras include a vast wall of whisky and live music several nights a week. (☎08-644 00 15; www.akkurat.se; Hornsgatan 18; ☺3pm-midnight Mon, to 1am Tue-Sat, 6pm-1am Sun; 🚇Slussen)

Himlen
COCKTAIL BAR

11 Map p74, E4

Cruise up the elevator to this elegant cocktail bar on the dizzying heights of the 26th floor; this is easily the the tallest building in Södermalm. After you have finished ogling the view, indulge in a fabulous cocktail, accompanied by oysters (175kr for six). There's also more formal dining in the 25th-floor restaurant (closed July and August). (☎08-660 60 68; www.restaurang himlen.se; Götgatan 78, Skrapan, 26th fl; ☺4pm-midnight Mon, to 1am Tue-Thu, to 3am Fri & Sat; 🛜; 🚇Medborgarplatsen)

Debaser Strand
BAR

12 Map p74, A2

Located in trendy Hornstull, Debaser is a Mexican restaurant, bar, nightclub and live-music venue all rolled into one – it's a key draw to this area. The Brooklyn Bar is a comfy hang-out, and a good place to catch live music or DJ sets. (☎08-658 63 50; www.debaser. se; Hornstulls Strand 4; ☺restaurant 5-11pm Tue-Thu, to 1am Fri & Sat, 11am-4pm Sun, bar Fri & Sat 4pm-3am; 🚇Hornstull)

Nada
BAR

13 Map p74, F4

With its soft orange glow, mini chandelier and decadent black-toned back bar, this cosy establishment pulls Söder's 20- and 30-something party people. Nightly, DJs play everything from alternative pop to '80s retro, while behind the bar mixologists sling elaborate summery cocktails. (☎08-644 70 20; Åsögatan 140; ☺5pm-1am Mon-Sat; 🚇Medborgarplatsen)

Local Life
Stockholm Vintage

A local fave among Södermalm's stylish thrift shops (there are quite a few!), **Lisa Larsson Second Hand** (Map p74, G4, 📞08-643 61 53; Bondegatan 48; ⏰1-6pm Tue-Fri, 11am-3pm Sat; 🚇Medborgarplatsen) is a small space packed with treasures dating from the '30s to the '70s. Look for leather jackets, handbags, shoes and vintage dresses.

Entertainment

Södra Teatern   THEATRE, LIVE MUSIC

14 ⭐ Map p74, E2

Accessible from Mosebacketorg and adjoining Mosebacke Etablissement, up the winding streets of old Södermalm, Södra Teatern is the original multifunctional event space, with its assortment of bars, stages and a restaurant. Whether you're relaxing in the beer garden or simply soaking up the ornate decor, this is a great place to dine and dance, or mingle with locals. Check the website for upcoming events. (📞08-53 19 94 90; www.sodrateatern.com; Mosebacketorg 1; ⏰8am-4pm Mon & Tue, to 11pm Wed & Thu, to 2am Fri, 11.30am-2am Sat, noon-4pm Sun; 🚇Slussen)

Mosebacke Etablissement   LIVE MUSIC

15 ⭐ Map p74, E2

Eclectic theatre and club nights aside, this historic culture palace hosts a mixed line-up of live music. Tunes span anything from home-grown pop to Antipodean rock. The outdoor terrace (featured in the opening scene of August Strindberg's novel *The Red Room*) combines dazzling city views with a thumping summertime bar. It adjoins Södra Teatern and a couple of other bars. (http://sodrateatern.com; Mosebacketorg 3; ⏰6pm-late; 🚇Slussen)

Zinkensdamms Idrottsplats   SPECTATOR SPORT

16 ⭐ Map p74, A3

Watching a bandy match is great fun. A precursor to ice hockey but with more players (11 to a side) and less fighting, the sport has grown massively popular since the rise of the Hammarby team in the late '90s. The season lasts from November to March; you can buy tickets at the gate. (www.svenskbandy.se/stockholm; Ringvägen 16; tickets around 130kr; 🚇Zinkensdamm)

Folkoperan   THEATRE

17 ⭐ Map p74, B2

Folkoperan gives opera a thoroughly modern overhaul with its intimate, cutting-edge and sometimes controversial productions. The under-26s enjoy half-price tickets. The attached restaurant-bar draws a loyal crowd on its own. (📞08-616 07 50; www.folkoperan.se; Hornsgatan 72; tickets 145-455kr; 🚇Zinkensdamm)

Shopping

English Bookshop

BOOKS

18 🔒 Map p74, F4

Excellent bookshop with secondhand and new titles, storytelling for kids, regular book signings (including Nell Zink of *The Wallcreeper* fame), writing workshops and plenty of seating space for perusing the pages. (📞08-790 55 10; Södermannagatan 22; ⏱10am-6.30pm Mon-Fri, to 5pm Sat, noon-3pm Sun; 🚇Medgorbarplatsen)

DesignTorget

DESIGN

19 🔒 Map p74, E3

If you love good design but don't own a Gold Amex, head to this chain, which sells the work of emerging designers alongside established denizens. There are several other locations, including one right next to the main tourist information office in Sergels Torg. (www.designtorget.se; Götgatan 31; ⏱10am-7pm Mon-Fri, 10am-6pm Sat, 11am-5.30pm Sun; 🚇Slussen)

Smiley Vintage

VINTAGE

20 🔒 Map p74, F3

This clever vintage shop remakes old clothes into new designs – no two items are alike. (Södermannagatan 14; ⏱11am-4.30pm Mon-Fri, 11.30am-5pm Sat, noon-4pm Sun; 🚇Medborgarplatsen)

PETER FORSBERG/SHOPPING/ALAMY STOCK PHOTO ©

DesignTorget

Judits

VINTAGE

21 🔒 Map p74, A2

A highly curated and well-loved secondhand clothing store, Judits carries premier brands and organises them beautifully, creating the effect of a clothing museum. It's a fun place to browse even if your budget doesn't quite stretch far enough for a vintage Acne jacket. (📞08-84 45 10; www.judits.se; Hornsgatan 75; ⏱11am-6.30pm Mon-Fri, to 4.30pm Sat Sep-May, 11am-6pm Mon-Fri, to 4pm Sat Jun-Aug; 🚇Zinkensdamm)

Explore

Östermalm

Östermalm is indisputably Stockholm's party district, where the beautiful, rich and famous come to play. It's also home to some of the city's best places to eat, drink and shop. But it isn't strictly about hedonism: this is also where you'll find two excellent history museums.

The Sights in a Day

☀️ Start your day with a visit to the engrossing **Historiska Museet** (p84), where you'll come face to face with episodes from Sweden's exciting history – and prehistory. It's a good-sized museum, so allow a couple of hours to really explore the place.

☀️ Take a break for lunch at the equally enthralling **Östermalms Saluhall** (p90), a gourmet food hall in a historic building. From fresh produce, fish and meat to imported cheeses and exotic pastries, the market stalls sell just about everything. In between the counters are a number of excellent cafes where you can grab a bite.

🌙 After lunch, visit the sobering **Armémuseum** (p90) for a lesson in war history. Walk it off with some window-shopping and a latte at **Sturekatten** (p92). Stop in for a decadent seafood dinner at **Sturehof** (p91), then fashionable drinks at **Lilla Baren at Riche** (p92).

For a local's day in Östermalm, see p86.

Top Sight

 Historiska Museet (p84)

🔍 Local Life

Opulent Östermalm (p86)

💜 Best of Stockholm

Eating
Ekstedt (p90)
Sturekatten (p92)

Museums & Galleries
Historiska Museet (p84)

Nightlife
Sturecompagniet (p92)
Spy Bar (p92)

Design
Svenskt Tenn (p93)
Nordiska Galleriet (p93)

Architecture
Dramaten (p93)
Östermalms Saluhall (p90)

Getting There

Ⓜ **Metro** (Tunnelbana) Östermalmstorg or Kungsträdgården to reach Östermalm; Gärdet to reach Ladugårdsgärdet

🚊 **Tram** 7, Nybroplan;

🚌 **Bus** 69

Top Sights
Historiska Museet

Sweden's national historical collection awaits at this enthralling museum. From Iron Age skates and a Viking boat to medieval textiles and Renaissance triptychs, it spans over 10,000 years of Swedish culture and history. There's an exhibit about the medieval Battle of Gotland (1361), an excellent multimedia display on the Vikings, a room of breathtaking altarpieces from the Middle Ages, a vast textile collection and a section on prehistoric culture.

◉ Map p88, H4

☎ 08-51 95 56 20

www.historiska.se

Narvavägen 13-17; free

⊙ 10am-5pm Jun-Aug, 11am-5pm Tue-Sun, to 8pm Wed Sep-May

🚌 44,56, 🚌 Djurgårdsbron, 🚇 Karlaplan, Östermalmstorg

Viking jewellery

Gold Room

The subterranean Gold Room is an undisputed highlight, a dimly lit chamber gleaming with Viking plunder and other treasures, including the jewel-encrusted Reliquary of St Elisabeth (who died at 24 and was canonised in 1235). The most astonishing artefacts are the three 5th-century gold collars discovered in Västergötland in the 19th century. The largest consists of seven rings, weighs 823g and is decorated with 458 symbolic figures.

Tapestries

The museum is known for its large collection of medieval textiles, including several that would have been displayed in very early wooden churches in northern Swedish villages.

Vikings

The museum's impressive Viking-era exhibition attempts to correct popular misconceptions about the Vikings and their age, focusing on their work as traders and on the lives of ordinary folk in those days (which, it turns out, was not all longboats and pillaging – most people were farmers). It's also a good place to learn about the rune stones that are still found scattered randomly across Sweden.

Battle of Gotland

One exhibit brings to life the medieval Battle of Gotland, which in 1361 pitted the island's farmers against professional soldiers in the Danish army. Needless to say it did not go well for the farmers: some 1800 were thrown into mass graves outside Visby. Archaeological studies have led to a clearer picture of what happened, and the display, though gruesome, is fascinating.

☑ **Top Tips**

▶ The galleries are divided by era: the upper floor holds the Middle Ages and baroque; the main (ground) floor is dedicated to prehistory; while downstairs is the Gold Room, with treasures from prehistory to medieval times.

▶ Captions in English describe the treasures and displays, and offer insights into each item's history and how it was made.

✗ **Take a Break**

There's a coffee shop and cafe near the entrance, with pleasant courtyard seating during summer. For something outside the museum, head up Linnégatan for Thai food in a vivid setting at Sabai-Soong (p92).

Local Life
Opulent Östermalm

Östermalm has come quite a long way from its early days as a cattle field. Now one of the wealthiest areas of Stockholm, its elegant buildings, lush parks and classy shops make it a dream to wander through. The addresses in this part of town may be exclusive, but its beauty is here for everyone to enjoy.

❶ **Kungliga Biblioteket**

Sweden's national library, Kungliga Biblioteket is beautifully situated in **Humlegården**, a leafy green park that acts as a neighbourhood oasis. The library holds a copy of virtually everything printed in Sweden or Swedish since 1661 (though it also has several much older items, including the 13th-century 'Devil's Bible').

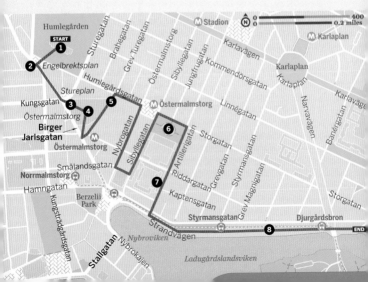

2 Vassa Eggen

If you've started your day in the local fashion – that is, none too early – it's probably getting close to lunchtime. Treat yourself to the surprisingly affordable weekday lunch (145kr) at steakhouse **Vassa Eggen** (☑08-21 61 69; www.vassaeggen.com; Birger Jarlsgatan 29; mains 225-450kr; ◷11.30am-2pm Mon-Fri, 5.30-10pm Mon, to midnight Tue-Thu, to 2am Fri & Sat; ☒Östermalmstorg), a longstanding neighbourhood favourite with a domed dining room, floor-to-ceiling wall murals and edgy bar.

3 Svampen

Built in 1937, then smashed and re-built in the '80s, this oddball structure (pictured on p82) – originally meant to be rain protection – has become a landmark and one of the most popular places to meet people before heading out on the town. (*Svampen* means 'the Mushroom', by the way.)

4 Sturegallerian

Home to dozens of high-end boutiques as well as the exclusive and historic spa **Sturebadet** (☑08-54 50 15 00; www.sturebadet.se; Sturegallerian 36, Stureplan; day pass from 595kr; ◷6.30am-10pm Mon-Fri, 8.30am-8.30pm Sat & Sun; ☒Östermalmstorg), this is not your average shopping mall, with interiors built to blend with the 19th-century facade.

5 Grev Turegatan

This pedestrianised shopping and dining street, along with Nybrogatan which runs parallel to the east, forms the core of the district – a highly concentrated dose of what Östermalm does best, with one-of-a-kind retail shops and sophisticated eateries set among beautiful apartment buildings with elaborately decorated exteriors.

6 Hedvig Eleonora Kyrka

This pretty, octagonal **church** (☑08-54 56 75 70; www.hedvigeleonora.se; Storgatan 2; admission free; ◷11am-6pm; ☒Östermalmstorg), consecrated in 1737, was initially designed by Jean de la Vallée in the 1660s as a private church for the Swedish Navy. The impressive pulpit was designed by Jean Eric Rehn, and the organ still has its original 1762 facade, by Carl Fredrik Aldencrantz. Check noticeboards for performance info.

7 Kungliga Hovstallet

The 1894 Royal Stables occupy an enormous red-brick building that extends for most of a block. The stables are part museum, part workplace – all royal-family transportation is arranged here, and the building holds 18 of the king's horses, as well as antique carriages and royal cars.

8 Strandvägen

Probably the fanciest boulevard in the city, it also provides a stunning view across the water to the city skyline. Lined with proud houses sporting fairy-tale turrets, the street is nearly 80m wide, with a row of trees down the centre, making for quiet strolling.

For reviews see

◉	Top Sights	p84
◉	Sights	p90
✖	Eating	p90
🍷	Drinking	p92
✪	Entertainment	p93
🔒	Shopping	p93

E F G H

Östermalmsgatan

0 — 200 m
0 — 0.1 miles

Stadion Ⓜ

Karlavägen

Karlavägen

Skeppargatan

Grevgatan

Karlaplan
Ⓜ Värtavägen

Karlaplan

1

Sibyllegatan

Jungfrugatan

Nybergsgatan

Kommendörsgatan

Karlaplan

Lützengatan

2

✕**8**

Linnégatan

Gumshornsgatan

Karlaplan

Karlavägen

3

Banérgatan

Storgatan

✕**4**

Skeppargatan

Grevgatan

Styrmansgatan

Grev Magnigatan

Historiska
Museet ⊙

Narvavägen

Narvavägen

4

Kaptensgatan

Torstensonsgatan

Banérgatan

Riddargatan

5

Grevgatan

Styrmangatan Ⓡ

Strandvägen

Djurgårdsbron

Strandvägen

Sights

Armémuseum
MUSEUM

1 Map p88, D3

Delve into the darker side of human nature at Armémuseum, where three levels of engrossing exhibitions explore the horrors of war through art, weaponry and life-size reconstructions of charging horsemen, forlorn barracks and starving civilians. You can even hop on a replica sawhorse for a taste of medieval torture. (Artillery Museum; ☎08-51 95 63 00; www.armemuseum.se; Riddargatan 13; admission free; ⏰10am-7pm Jun-Aug, 11am-8pm Tue, 11am-5pm Wed-Sun Sep-May; ⊠Östermalmstorg)

Naturhistoriska Riksmuseet
MUSEUM

2 Map p88, A1

A fantastic place to bring kids, the Natural History Museum has seen a lot of changes since Carl von Linné

> ☑ Top Tip
> **Budget Bites**
> In need of a rapid-fire lunch that won't break the bank? The cafes and food counters inside **Östermalms Saluhall** (Map p88, E3, www.saluhallen.com; Östermalmstorg; admission free; ⏰9.30am-7pm Mon-Fri, to 5pm Sat; ⊠Östermalmstorg) make for an above-average yet still quick and generally budget-friendly lunch stop.

founded it in 1739. These days, everything is interactive: you can crawl inside a human ear, sit through a forest fire or step into a chamber that mimics a swarm of mosquitoes. Of course, there are still countless displays of fossils, rock specimens, and whole forests' worth of taxidermied wildlife, marine life and the hardy fauna of the polar regions. (Swedish Museum of Natural History; ☎08-51 95 40 00; www.nrm.se; Frescativägen 40; admission free; ⏰10am-6pm Tue-Sun, open select Mon; P🚻; ⊠Universitetet)

Eating

Ekstedt
SWEDISH $$$

3 Map p88, C2

Dining here is as much an experience as a meal. Chef Niklas Ekstedt's education in French and Italian cooking informs his approach to traditional Scandinavian cuisine – but only slightly. Choose from a four- or six-course set menu built around reindeer and pike-perch. Everything is cooked in a wood-fired oven, over a fire pit or smoked in a chimney. (☎08-611 12 10; http://ekstedt.nu/en; Humlegårdsgatan 17; 4/6 courses 890/1090kr; ⏰from 6pm Tue-Thu, from 5pm Fri, from 4pm Sat; ⊠Östermalmstorg)

Gastrologik
SWEDISH $$$

4 Map p88, E4

Gastrologik is at the forefront of dynamic and modern Scandinavian cooking. Diners choose from a set three- or six-course menu, which changes frequently, as the chefs work closely with suppliers to deliver the freshest and most readily available produce with a nod to sustainability and tradition. Reservations are essential. (☏08-662 30 60; www.gastrologik.se; Artillerigatan 14; tasting menu 1595kr; ☺6-11.30pm Tue-Fri, 5-11.30pm Sat; ☒Östermalmstorg)

Sturehof
SEAFOOD $$$

5 ✖ Map p88, B3

Superb for late-night sipping and supping, this convivial brasserie sparkles with gracious staff, celebrity regulars and fabulous seafood-centric dishes (the bouillabaisse is brilliant). Both the front and back bars are a hit with the eye-candy brigade and perfect for a postmeal flirt. (☏08-440 57 30; www.sturehof.com; Stureplan 2; mains 185-495kr; ☺11am-2am; ☒Östermalmstorg)

Café Saturnus
CAFE $

6 ✖ Map p88, A1

For velvety caffè latte, Gallic-inspired baguettes and perfect pastries, saunter into this casually chic bakery-cafe. Sporting a stunning mosaic floor, stripy wallpaper and a few outdoor tables, it's a fabulous spot to flick through the paper while tackling what has to be Stockholm's most enormous sweet roll (cinnamon or cardamom, take your pick). (☏08-611 77 00; Eriksbergsgatan 6; sweet

Armémuseum (Artillery Museum)

rolls 50kr, salads & sandwiches 68-138kr; ☺8am-8pm Mon-Fri, 9am-7pm Sat & Sun; ☒2 Eriksbergsgatan)

Lisa Elmqvist
SEAFOOD $$

7 ✖ Map p88, D3

Seafood fans, look no further. This Stockholm legend is never short of a satisfied lunchtime crowd. The menu changes daily, so let the waiters order for you; classics include shrimp sandwiches and a gravadlax plate. There's also an excellent selection of wine. (☏08-55 34 04 10; www.lisaelmqvist.se; Östermalmstorg, Östermalms Saluhall; mains from 215kr; ☺11am-11pm Mon-Sat; ☒Östermalmstorg)

Sabai-Soong

THAI **$$**

8 Map p88, F2

Super-kitsch Sabai-Soong is keeping it real despite the snooty address. A hit with families and fashionistas alike, its tropical-trash day-glo interior is the perfect place to chow down on simple and faithful versions of *tod man pla* and fiery green curry. (☑08-663 12 77; www.sabai.se; Linnégatan 39B; ◷11am-2pm Mon-Fri, 5-10pm daily; ⍳Östermalmstorg)

Sturekatten

CAFE **$**

9 Map p88, C3

Looking like a life-size doll's house, this vintage cafe is a fetching blend of antique chairs, oil paintings, ladies who lunch and servers in black-and-white garb. Slip into a salon chair, pour some tea and nibble on a piece of apple pie or a *kanelbulle* (cinnamon bun). (☑08-611 16 12; www.sturekatten.se;

Understand
Good Water

You'll see signs in many Stockholm hotels boasting that the city's tap water is among the cleanest on Earth and perfectly good to drink. Stockholm's water comes from Lake Mälaren in the middle of the city, itself clean enough that locals swim in it all summer and fish from it year-round. There's no excuse for buying bottled water here: carry your own refillable water bottle and don't hesitate to fill it from the tap.

Riddargatan 4; pastries from 35kr; ◷9am-7pm Mon-Fri, 9am-6pm Sat, 10am-6pm Sun; ⍳Östermalmstorg)

Drinking

Lilla Baren at Riche

BAR

10 Map p88, C4

A darling of Östermalm's hip parade, this pretty, glassed-in bar mixes smooth bar staff, skilled DJs and a packed crowd of fashion-literate media types; head in by 9pm to score a seat. (☑08-54 50 35 60; Birger Jarlsgatan 4; ◷5pm-2am Tue-Sat; ⍳Östermalm)

Sturecompagniet

CLUB

11 Map p88, B3

Swedish soap stars, flowing champagne and look-at-me attitude set a decadent scene at this glitzy, mirrored and becurtained hallway. Dress to impress and flaunt your wares to commercial house. Big-name guest DJs come through frequently. (☑08-54 50 76 00; www.sturecompagniet.se; Stureplan 4; ◷10pm-3am Thu-Sat; ⍳Östermalmstorg)

Spy Bar

CLUB

12 Map p88, B2

Though it's no longer the super-hip star of the scene it once was, the Spy Bar (aka 'the Puke'; *spy* means vomit in Swedish) is still a landmark and fun to check out if you're making the Östermalm rounds. It covers three levels in a turn-of-the-century flat (spot the tile stoves). (Birger Jarlsgatan

Nocturnal Scenes

The streets branching off from Östermalmstorg hold some of the city's primo nightclubs as well as mellower terrace bars – ideal for a bit of people-watching (most of them are pretty attractive around here).

20; cover from 160kr; ⊙10pm-5am Wed-Sat; 🚇Östermalmstorg)

Entertainment

Dramaten   THEATRE

13 Map p88, C4

The Royal Theatre stages a range of plays in a sublime art-nouveau environment. You can also take a guided tour in English at 4pm most days (adult/child 30/60kr), bookable online. Half-price tickets may be available an hour before showtime, for those willing to gamble. (Kungliga Dramatiska Teatern; ☎08-667 06 80; www. dramaten.se; Nybroplan; tickets 150-450kr; 🚇Kungsträdgården)

Shopping

Svenskt Tenn   ARTS, HOMEWARES

14 🏠 Map p88, D5

As much a museum of design as an actual shop, this iconic store is home to the signature fabrics and furniture of Josef Frank and his contemporaries. Browsing here is a great way to get a quick handle on what people mean by 'classic Swedish design' – and it's owned by a foundation that contributes heavily to arts funding. (☎08-670 16 00; www.svenskttenn.se; Nybrogatan 15; ⊙10am-6pm Mon-Fri, 10am-4pm Sat; 🚇Kungsträdgården)

Nordiska Galleriet   ARTS & CRAFTS

15 🏠 Map p88, D3

This sprawling showroom is a design freak's El Dorado – think Hannes Wettstein chairs, Hella Jongerius sofas, Alvar Aalto vases and mini Verner Panton chairs for style-sensitive kids. Luggage-friendly options include designer coat-hangers, glossy architecture books and bright Marimekko paper napkins. (☎08-442 83 60; www. nordiskagalleriet.se; Nybrogatan 11; ⊙10am-6pm Mon-Fri, to 5pm Sat; 🚇Östermalmstorg)

Rönnells Antikvariat   BOOKS

16 🏠 Map p88, A1

From vintage Astrid Lindgren books to dusty 19th-century travel guides, the 100,000-strong collection of books here, many in English, make this one of the meatiest secondhand bookshops in town. Forage through the sales rack for a new dog-eared friend. (☎08-54 50 15 60; www.ronnells.se; Birger Jarlsgatan 32; ⊙10am-6pm Mon-Fri, noon-4pm Sat; 🚇Östermalmstorg)

Top Sights
Millesgården

Getting There

Millesgården is on the island of Lidingö, 7km northeast of the city centre.

Ⓜ (Tunnelbana) Ropsten, then bus 207

From 1906 to 1931, Millesgården was the home and studio of sculptor Carl Milles (1875–1955), whose delicate water sprites and other whimsical sculptures dot the city. The artist's delightful personality, which is clearly evident in his sculptures, also imbues the house where he lived and worked. It's an inspiring place to visit, especially for anyone interested in art and design.

Sculptures by Carl Miles

Art Gallery

The grounds include a crisp modern gallery in neoclassical style for changing exhibitions of contemporary art. Carl and Olga Milles themselves laid the tiles for the intricate black-and-white mosaic floor.

Sculpture Park

Milles transformed the rough hillside of the property into an exquisite outdoor sculpture garden, where items from ancient Greece, Rome, medieval times and the Renaissance intermingle with his own creations. Seek out 'Little Austria', a garden space Milles designed for his wife to ease her homesickness. Most of the garden is arranged to evoke the Mediterranean coast.

Little Studio

Inside the sculpture park, the Little Studio, built by Milles' brother Evert, contains a fresco painting of the Bay of Naples. Black-and-white marble paths bordered by pines and birches, and crowned with Italianate columns, lead the way to the studio. The studio was initially built to improve the state of Milles' lungs, which suffered from the dust his work created.

Milles' Home

The artist couple visited Pompeii in 1921, and after this trip they started adding elaborate Pompeian touches to the decor – especially in what became the Red Room, with its mosaic floors and frescoed walls. Olga painted the kitchen cabinets after the Delft ceramic-tiled walls. The Music Room contains not only a grand piano but also a Donatello sculpture and a Canaletto painting, among other treasures.

☎ 08-446 75 90

www.millesgarden.se

Herserudsvägen 32

adult/child 150kr/free

🕐 11am-5pm, closed Mon Oct-Apr

🚇 Ropsten, then bus 201, 202, 204, 206, 207

☑ Top Tips

▶ From mid-June through August, a 30-minute guided introduction in English is included in the ticket price, starting at 1.15pm Tuesday and Thursday.

▶ Be sure to bring a good camera – the setting is very photogenic.

✗ Take a Break

Millesgården Lanthandel (mains 155-220kr) is a cafe/restaurant occupying the middle terrace of the Sculpture Park. It serves coffee, cakes, lunch and dinner either outdoors or inside by the fireplace in winter.

Local Life
Museums of Gärdet & Ladugårdsgärdet

Getting There

Gärdet and La-
dugårdsgärdet are
east of Östermalm.

M (Tunnelbana)
Gärdet, then bus 1 or
76 to Frihamnen for
Magasin 3

🚌 from Kaknästornet
take 69

These two conjoined parklike areas – one a casual suburban neighbourhood, the other a former royal playground that's now a wide-open green space – contain some of the best museums in the city. And they're much easier to reach than they may initially seem – a quick bus or tunnelbana trip, or a leisurely walk from Östermalm.

❶ Gärdet Tunnelbana Station

From the Gärdet tunnelbana station, walk south along Sandhamnsgatan through a quiet residential neighbourhood and onto the wide open field that is Ladugårdsgärdet. This is a great place for a picnic or a nap in the sun, or a jog if you're more ambitious.

❷ Sjöhistoriska Museet

At the southern edge of Ladugårdsgärdet, you'll find a trio of excellent kid-friendly museums. The smallest and cutest of the three is the nautical **Sjöhistoriska Museet** (National Maritime Museum; ☑08-519 549 00; Djurgårdsbrunnsvägen 24; admission free; ☉10am-5pm Tue-Sun; ☐69 Museiparken) – a must for fans of model ships (there are over 1500 mini vessels in the collection). The exhibits also explore Swedish shipbuilding, sailors and life on deck.

❸ Tekniska Museet

Tekniska (Museum of Science & Technology; ☑08-450 56 00; www.tekniskamuseet.se; Museivägen 7; adult/child 150/100kr, free 5-8pm Wed; ☉10am-5pm Thu-Tue, to 8pm Wed; ⛹; ☐69 Museiparken) is a vast museum full of interactive science and technology displays. You can test your balance, flexibility and strength with the kinetic experiments and exhibits in the huge 'Teknorama' room, and the museum also features a climate-change game, a model railway and an exhibition dedicated to inventions by women.

❹ Etnografiska Museet

Next door, the fascinating and atmospheric **Museum of Ethnography** (☑010-456 12 99; www.etnografiska.se; Djurgårdsbrunnsvägen 34; admission free; ☉11am-5pm Tue-Sun, to 8pm Wed; ☐69 Museiparken) stages evocative displays on various aspects of non-European cultures, including dynamic temporary exhibitions and frequent live performances. Recent examples include a display about the cultural treasures of Afghanistan, a look at gender norms, and 'real-life' voodoo. There's a good cafe, too.

❺ Kaknästornet

It's a nice walk to reach the big lookout tower that looms over this whole area. The 155m-tall **Kaknästornet** (www.kaknastornet.se; Mörka Kroken 28-30; adult/child 70/25kr; ☉10am-6pm Sun-Thu, to 9pm Fri & Sat; ☐69 Kaknästornet) is the automatic operations centre for radio and TV broadcasting in Sweden. Opened in 1967, it's among the tallest buildings in Scandinavia. There's a small visitor centre on the ground floor and an elevator up to the observation deck, restaurant and cafe near the top, from where there are stellar views of the city and archipelago.

Explore

Kungsholmen

Until recently something of an underappreciated gem, especially among visitors, Kungsholmen has really come into its own. Best explored on foot, this is a laid-back, mostly residential neighbourhood with great places to eat, kid-friendly parks and an amazingly long stretch of tree-lined waterside walking. Plus it's home to one of Stockholm's most important buildings, architecturally and practically, in the Stadshuset (City Hall).

The Sights in a Day

☀ Start your day with a waterside stroll down to **Stadshuset** (p104; pictured left) for a thorough tour – don't neglect to visit the tower.

☼ Spend the middle of the day wandering the area around Scheelegatan and Hantverkargatan in search of an inspiring lunch destination. You'll have plenty to choose from – this is a great neighbourhood for ethnic eateries, so opt for anything that strikes your fancy. **Bergamott** (p103) is an excellent choice. Don't be surprised if you're also tempted to do some window-shopping.

☾ Afterwards, walk off lunch along the water, following Norr Mälarstrand as far as you feel like going. Turn around and head back towards town, stopping for a leisurely drink and satisfying dinner at the exceptionally friendly and pretty floating restaurant **Mälarpaviljongen** (p103). Afterwards, **Lemon Bar** (p104), a laid-back neighbourhood hang-out, is perfect for a nightcap.

Top Sight

 Stadshuset (p100)

 Best of Stockholm

Nightlife
Lemon Bar (p104)

Shopping
Västermalmsgallerian (p107)

Fashion
59 Vintage Store (p104)

Architecture
Stadshuset (p104)

Parks
Rålambshovsparken (p103)

Getting There

Ⓜ **Metro** (Tunnelbana) Rådhuset, Fridhemsplan

🚶 **Walk** It's a short walk across Stadshusbron from the area around Centralstationen

Top Sights
Stadshuset

The mighty Stadshuset (City Hall) dominates Stockholm. It looks stern and weighty from afar, but inside it's secretly aglitter. Built of about eight million bricks, it was designed by architect Ragnar Östberg, a proponent of the Swedish National Romantic style, and opened in 1923. Aside from serving as a striking landmark, it holds the offices of more than 200 government workers, as well as its better-known banquet halls and courtyards.

Map p102, E4

www.stockholm.se/stad shuset; Hantverkargatan 1

adult/child 100/50kr, tower 50kr/free

9am-3.30pm, admission by tour only

3, 62 Stadshuset, Rådhuset

Golden Hall

The Tower

Atop the building's 106m-high tower is a golden spire featuring the heraldic symbol of Swedish power: the three royal crowns. Entry is by guided tour only; tours in English take place every 30 to 40 minutes between 9.30am and 4pm in summer, and less frequently during the rest of the year. There are stellar views and it's a great thigh workout.

Golden Hall

Nestled in the centre of Stadshuset is the glittering, mosaic-lined *Gyllene salen* (Golden Hall). The beguiling mosaics, made from 19 million bits of gold leaf, are by Einar Forseth (1892–1988). The post-Nobel banquet dancing and festivities happen here.

Prins Eugen's Fresco

Prins Eugen, who became a successful artist and was a generous patron of the arts, donated his own fresco painting of the lake view from the gallery, *The City on the Water,* which can be seen along one wall in the Prince's Gallery. Along the other wall are windows opening on to an impressive real-life version of the city on the water.

Stadshusparken

Don't neglect the lovely park abreast of Stadshuset, pretty in all seasons, with its views of Riddarholmen across the water. Two statues by Carl Eldh guard the steps, and Christian Eriksson's *Engelbrekt the Freedom Fighter* graces a pillar in the corner of the park. If the weather's warm, do as Stockholmers do and take a swim or sunbathe on the concrete platform.

☑ Top Tips

▸ Note that the tower and tower museum are only open for visits from May through September.

▸ If you're not sure you're up for walking 106m worth of stairs, there's an elevator that will take you halfway to the top.

✗ Take a Break

You can dine like a Nobel Prize winner in Stadshuset's basement restaurant, **Stadshuskällaren** (www.stadshuskallarensthlm.se). Regular mains (285kr to 310kr) are mostly hearty traditional meat-and-veg courses; groups can order the Nobel Menu (1865kr) from any year they like, served on Nobel porcelain. Reservations are recommended.

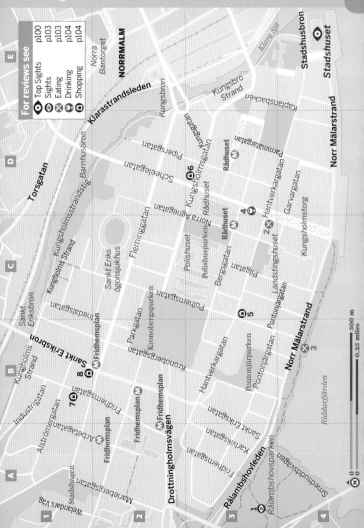

NORRMALM

Torsgatan

Klarastrandsleden

Stadshuset

Norr Mälarstrand

Norra Bantorget

Kungsbron

Kungsbro Strand

Kaplansbacken

Kungsholmsstrandstig

Barnhusbron

Pipersgatan

Scheelegatan

Kungsgatan

Parmmätargatan

Rådhuset

Stadshusbron

Sankt Eriksbron

Kungsholms Strand

Lindhagensgatan

Sankt Eriks ögonsjukhus

Fleminggatan

Kungsholmsgatan

Norra Agnegatan

Rådhuset

Hantverkargatan

Garvargatan

Kungsholmstorg

Polishuset

Polishusparken

Bergsgatan

Landstingshuset

Pilgatan

Pontonjärgatan

Industrigatan

Kungsholms Strand

Fridhemsplan

Sankt Eriksplan

Fridhemsgatan

Polhemsgatan

Kronobergsparken

Kronobergsgatan

Parkgatan

Hantverkargatan

Pontonjärparken

Pontonjärgatan

Pontonjärgatan

Norr Mälarstrand

Riddarfjärden

Alströmergatan

Arbetargatan

Fridhemsplan

Fridhemsplan

Fridhemsvägen

Drottningholmsvägen

Fridhemsgatan

Karlbergsvägen

Sankt Eriksgatan

Karlviksgatan

Welanders Väg

Stadshagen

Marieberggatan

Rålambshovsleden

Rålambshovsparken

Rålambshovsvägen

Smedsuddsvägen

Smedsuddsvägen

500 m

0.25 miles

Kungsholmen skyline

Sights

Rålambshovsparken
PARK

1  Map p102, A3

In summer, Rålambshovsparken is one of the city's favourite playgrounds. Take a swim, hire a canoe or join in the free alfresco aerobics sessions usually held on summer nights. (🚶; 🚇Fridhemsplan)

Eating

Bergamott
FUSION $$$

2 Map p102, C3

The very cool French chefs in this kitchen don't simply whip up

to-die-for French-Italian dishes, they'll probably deliver them to your table, talk you through the produce and guide you through the wine list. It's never short of a convivial crowd, so it's best to book, especially when jazz musicians drop in for a soulful evening jam. Menu changes daily. (📞08-650 30 34; www.restaurang bergamott.se; Hantverkargatan 35; mains 195-325kr; ⏱5.30pm-midnight Tue-Sat; 🚇Rådhuset)

Mälarpaviljongen
SWEDISH, AMERICAN $$

3 Map p102, B4

When the sun's out, few places beat this alfresco waterside spot for some

Local Life

Street Eats

There are plenty of interesting places to eat in Kungsholmen, but you'll find a particularly good and varied range of eateries along **Scheelegatan** and **Hantverkargatan**, where the two streets intersect (Map p102, D3). And as always in Stockholm, the people-watching/admiration here is part of the street experience.

Nordic dolce vita. Its glassed-in gazebo, vast floating terraces and surrounding herb gardens are only upstaged by the lovely and supremely welcoming service. Both food and cocktails are beautified versions of the classics: meatballs, fried herring, gravadlax, and the like. Opening times vary with the weather. (☑08-650 87 01; www.malarpaviljongen.se; Norr Mälarstrand 63; mains 185-225kr; ⏱11am-1am; ⌷Rådhuset)

Drinking

Lemon Bar   BAR

4 📍 Map p102, D3

A favourite among locals for its laid-back vibe, the Lemon Bar epitomises the kind of comfy neighbourhood joint you can drop into on the spur of the moment and count on finding a friendly crowd and good music, mostly Swedish pop hits that may or may not result in dancing. (☑08-650 17 78; www.lemonbar.se; Scheelegatan 8; ⏱5pm-1am Tue, to 3am Wed-Sat; Ⓜ Rådhuset)

Shopping

59 Vintage Store   CLOTHING

5 🔒 Map p102, C3

This rack-packed nirvana of retro threads will have you playing dress-up for hours. Both girls and boys can expect high-quality gear from the 1950s to the 1970s, including glam, midcentury ballgowns, platform boots, Brit-pop blazers, *Dr Zhivago* faux-fur hats and the odd sequinned sombrero. (☑08-652 37 27; www.59vintagestore.se; Hantverkargatan 59; ⏱11am to 6pm Mon-Fri, 11am-4pm Sat; ⌷Rådhuset)

Frank Form   CLOTHING

6 🔒 Map p102, D3

Fetching interior design, fashion and jewellery you're unlikely to find elsewhere in town, including pieces from the UK, Spain and the Czech Republic. Pick up slinky guys' sweaters from Basque label Loreak Mendian, a classic handbag from Irish designer Orla Kiely or one-off jewellery from Swedish designer Jezebel, commissioned specially for the store. (☑08-54 55 05 00; www.frankform.se; Kungsholmsgatan 20; ⏱11am-6.30pm Mon-Fri, to 5pm Sat; ⌷Rådhuset)

Understand

Viking History

Scandinavia's greatest impact on world history probably occurred during the Viking Age (late 8th into the mid-11th century) when hardy pagan Norsemen set sail for other shores. The Swedish Vikings were more inclined towards trade than their Norwegian or Danish counterparts, but their reputation as fearsome warriors was fully justified. At home it was the height of paganism; Viking leaders claimed descent from Freyr, 'God of the World', and celebrations at Uppsala involved human sacrifices.

Long-Distance Raiders

The Vikings sailed fast manoeuvrable boats, sturdy enough for ocean crossings. Initial hit-and-run raids along the European coast were followed by military expeditions, settlement and trade. The Vikings visited the Slavic heartland (giving it the name 'Rus'), and ventured as far as Newfoundland, Constantinople (Istanbul) and Baghdad.

Christianity Arrives

Christianity only took hold when Sweden's first Christian king, Olof Skötkonung (c 968–1020), was baptised. However, by 1160, King Erik Jedvarsson (Sweden's patron saint, St Erik) had virtually destroyed the last remnants of Viking paganism.

In a Word

The word 'Viking' is derived from *vik*, meaning bay or cove – probably a reference to Vikings' anchorages during raids. The root word appears in many Swedish place names – Örnsköldsvik, in northern Sweden, for example; or Alvik, a Stockholm tunnelbana stop.

Learn More about the Vikings

The Vikings by Magnus Magnusson covers their achievements in Scandinavia (including Sweden), as well as their wild deeds around the world. The Unesco World Heritage Viking trading centre of **Birka** (www.birkavikingastaden.se/en; Björkö; adult/child 395/198kr; ⊙May-Sep; 🚢Stromma), on Björkö in Lake Mälaren, offers an up-close look at Viking history. **Strömma Kanalbolaget** (www.stromma.se) runs cruises.

Understand

Essential Swedish Reads

One of the best ways to get inside the collective mind of a country is to read its top authors – here's a Swedish fiction primer:

Popular Works

Famous books by Swedish authors include *The Long Ships* (1954) by Frans Gunnar Bengtsson, *The Wonderful Adventures of Nils* (1906–07) by Selma Lagerlöf, the *Emigrants* series (1949–59) by Vilhelm Moberg, *Marking* (1963–64) by Dag Hammarskjöld, *Röda Rummet* (1879) by August Strindberg, *The Evil* (1981) by Jan Guillou and, more recently, *A Man Called Ove* (2013) by Fredrik Backman.

Crime Fiction

It's the country's detective fiction that has drawn the most attention recently, however. The massive success of the *Millennium Trilogy*, by the late Stieg Larsson, has brought well-deserved attention to the genre. *The Girl with the Dragon Tattoo* (2005) is the tip of the iceberg when it comes to this genre.

Other names to look for include Håkan Nesser, whose early novels *The Mind's Eye* (1993) and *Woman with Birthmark* (1996) have recently been translated into English; and Sweden's best-known crime fiction writer, Henning Mankell, whose novels featured moody detective Kurt Wallander. Johan Theorin's quartet of mysteries (starting with *Echoes from the Dead*, 2008) is set on the island of Öland. Other writers include Karin Alvtegen (Sweden's 'queen of crime'), Kerstin Ekman, Camilla Läckberg and Jens Lapidus.

Grandpa ACCESSORIES, CLOTHING

7 🔒 Map p102, B1

With a design inspired by the hotels of the French Riviera during the '70s, Grandpa's second Stockholm location is crammed with atmosphere, as well as artfully chosen vintage and faux-vintage clothing, cool and quirky accessories and whatnots, random hairdryers, suitcases and old radios, plus a cool little cafe serving good espresso. (☎08-643 60 81; www.grandpa. se; Fridhemsgatan 43; ☺11am-7pm Mon-Fri, to 5pm Sat, noon-4pm Sun; 🚇Fridhemsplan)

Västermalmsgallerian SHOPPING CENTRE

8 🔒 Map p102, B1

This busy mall right outside the Fridhemsplan tunnelbana stop is home to some noteworthy residents. Pick up Scandi-design wares at DesignTorget, sexy Swedish briefs at BjörnBorg,

Local Life

Urban Beaches

Kungsholmen boasts the largest beach in the Stockholm city centre, called **Smedsuddsbadet**. At the first sign of warm weather in spring, locals flock here to soak up the sun after the long, dark Swedish winter. To find the beach, follow the footpath along Norr Mälarstrand west beside the water towards Rålambshovsparken (p103). Rålambshovsparken is also the place to join locals in whatever the latest exercise trend may be: outdoor yoga, aerobics, crossfit, bootcamp...you name it, they're into it.

cult cosmetics at Face Stockholm, and democratically priced kids' and women's threads at H&M. (☎08-737 20 00; www.vastermalmsgallerian.se; St Eriksgatan 45; ☺10am-7pm Mon-Fri, to 5pm Sat, 11am-5pm Sun; 🚇Fridhemsplan)

Top Sights
Drottningholm

Getting There

Drottningholm is 10km west of Stockholm.

Ⓜ Brommaplan, then bus 301–323.

⚓ Strömma Kanal-bolaget boats depart Stadshusbron in Stockholm (one hour one-way; 210kr return)

The royal residence and parks of Drottningholm on Lovön are justifiably popular attractions and easy to visit from the capital. Home to the royal family for part of the year, Drottningholm's Renaissance-inspired main palace was designed by architectural great Nicodemus Tessin the Elder and begun in 1662, about the same time as Versailles.

Hedvig Eleonora's State Bedchamber

Hedvig Eleonora's Bedchamber

The highly ornamented State Bedchamber of Hedvig Eleonora (1636–1715), consort of King Karl X Gustav, is Sweden's most expensive baroque interior. It's decorated with paintings featuring the childhood of their son, who would become King Karl XI. The painted ceiling shows the queen consort with her king.

Karl X Gustav Gallery

The Karl X Gustav Gallery, in baroque style, depicts this monarch's militaristic exploits – though the paintings on the ceiling are of classical battle scenes, lending their mythical heft to Karl X's persona.

Library

Although the bulk of Lovisa Ulrika's collection of 2000 books has been moved to the Royal Library in Stockholm for safekeeping, her library here is still a bright and impressive room, complete with most of its original 18th-century fittings.

Corps de Garde

The Lower North Corps de Garde was originally a guardroom, bare and functional, but as the need for armed guards just outside the door diminished, this room was repurposed and beautified. It's now replete with gilt-leather wall hangings, which used to feature in many palace rooms during the 17th century.

Staircase

The palace's elaborate staircase, with statues and trompe l'oeil embellishments at every turn, was the work of both Nicodemus Tessin the Elder and the Younger. The geometric gardens, angled to impress, are well worth exploring.

☎ 08-402 62 80

www.kungahuset.se

adult/child 130/65kr, combined ticket incl Kina Slott 190/90kr

🕐 10am-4.30pm May-Sep, 11am-3.30pm Oct & Apr, noon-3.30pm Sat & Sun rest of year (closed mid-Dec–Jan)

🚢 Stadshuskajen (summer only), 🚇 Brommaplan, then bus 301-323 Drottningholm

☑ Top Tips

▶ Explore on your own, or take a one-hour guided tour (30kr; in English at 10am, noon, 2pm and 4pm June to August, noon and 2pm other months).

✗ Take a Break

Bring a picnic and enjoy lunch in the gardens, or munch at one of the restaurants by the palace. **Cafe Drottningholm** (☎ 08-759 03 96; Kantongatan; waffles 65kr; 🕐 9am-4.30pm May-Sep) is a cute cafe next to Kina Slott (p110).

Understand
Hedvig Eleonora

The queen consort of King Karl X Gustav, Hedvig Eleonora was by all accounts a great beauty and a strong leader. After the king's death in 1660, she became regent until their son, Karl XI, came of age. When he died in 1697, she returned to that position, but only briefly, until her grandson, Karl XII, became king. Both son and grandson were devoted to Hedvig Eleonora and took her counsel seriously. Hers was an age of intrigue and gossip, rumoured affairs and various sordid alliances, both personal and political. She loved the theatre, had a gambling habit, and liked to party.

Drottningholms Slottsteater & Teatermuseum

Slottsteater (Court Theatre & Museum; www.dtm.se; entry by tour adult/child 100/70kr; ☺tours hourly noon-3.30pm Fri-Sun Oct & Apr, noon-3.30pm Sat & Sun Nov & Mar, 11am-4.30pm May-Aug, 11am-3.30pm Sep) was completed in 1766 on the instructions of Queen Lovisa Ulrika. Remarkably untouched from the time of Gustav III's death (1792) until 1922, it's now the oldest theatre in the world still in its original state. The fascinating guided tour takes you into other rooms in the building, where highlights include hand-painted 18th-century wallpaper and an Italianate room (salon de déjeuner) with fake three-dimensional wall effects and a ceiling that looks like the sky.

Performances are held at Drottningholms Slottsteater in summer using 18th-century machinery, including ropes, pulleys, wagons and wind machines. Scenes can be changed in less than seven seconds! Illusion was the order of the day, and accordingly the theatre makes use of fake marble, fake curtains and papier-mâché viewing boxes. Even the stage was designed to create illusions regarding size.

Kina Slott

At the far end of the royal gardens is **Kina Slott** (Chinese Pavilion; adult/child 100/50kr, combined ticket incl royal palace 190/90kr; ☺11am-4.30pm May-Sep), a lavishly decorated Chinese pavilion built by King Adolf Fredrik as a birthday surprise for Queen Lovisa Ulrika in 1753. Restored between 1989 and 1996, it boasts one of the finest rococo chinoiserie interiors in Europe. The admission price includes guided tours, which run at 11am, 1pm and 3pm daily from June to August (fewer in May and September).

Guards' Tent

On the slope below Kina Slott, the carnivalesque Guards' Tent was erected in 1781 as quarters for the dragoons of Gustav III, but it's not really a tent at all (another illusion).

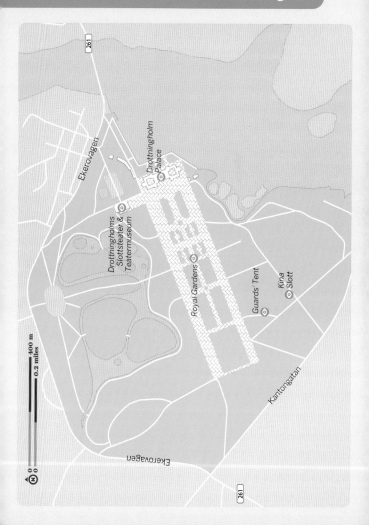

Drottningholm

Drottningholm
Palace

Ekerovägen

Drottningholms
Slottsteater &
Teatermuseum

Royal Gardens

Guards' Tent

Kina
Slott

Kantongatan

Ekerovägen

261

261

400 m
0.2 miles

N

Explore

Vasastan

This relaxed, residential neighbourhood has some of the best places to eat in Stockholm, along with several great hotels and a couple of slick art galleries in impressive buildings. It's also home to one of the greatest examples of Scandinavian architecture, Stadsbiblioteket. Wander around, take a nap in a park and join the laid-back locals in just hanging out.

The Sights in a Day

☀ Why not start your day with a coffee and pastry at the central and very unpretentious **Konditori Ritorno** (p117). Then hop across the park to **Sven-Harrys Konstmuseum** (p116), where temporary exhibits (including a bunch of Strindberg paintings) complement the building's sleek design.

☼ Grab lunch at cosy and comfortable **Vurma** (p117) or, if you're not in a big rush, stop in for an afternoon pint and some Swedish comfort food at the old beer hall **Tennstopet** (p119). Continue walking up along Odengatan for a view of the elegant public library, **Stadsbiblioteket** (p115), designed by noted Swedish architect Erik Gunnar Asplund.

☾ Meander over towards the impressively housed **Bonniers Konsthall** (p115; pictured left), designed by architect Johan Celsing and filled with enough shiny objects to occupy you until dinnertime. Your dining options in this neighbourhood are fantastic – if you're in the mood for upscale traditional Swedish cuisine with stellar presentation and top-notch service but an unfussy atmosphere, opt for **Tranan** (p116), a local favourite.

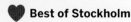 **Best of Stockholm**

Cafes
Caffé Nero (p116)

Museums & Galleries
Bonniers Konsthall (p115)

Architecture
Stadsbiblioteket (p115)

Parks
Vasaparken (p115)

Getting There

Ⓜ **Metro** (Tunnelbana) St Eriksplan, Odenplan, Rådmansgatan

Stadsbiblioteket (public library)

Sights

Bonniers Konsthall
GALLERY

1 ◎ Map p114, B4

This ambitious gallery keeps culture fiends busy with a fresh dose of international contemporary art, as well as a reading room, a fab cafe and a busy schedule of art seminars and artists-in-conversation sessions. The massive, transparent flatiron building was designed by Johan Celsing. There are discussions about the exhibitions in English at 1pm, 3pm, 5pm and 7pm Wednesdays, and 1pm and 4pm Thursday to Sunday. Curators lead free guided tours on Sunday at 2pm. (📞08-736 42 48; www.bonniers konsthall.se; Torsgatan 19; admission free; ⏱noon-5pm Thu-Sun, to 8pm Wed; 🚇St Eriksplan)

Stadsbiblioteket
LIBRARY

2 ◎ Map p114, D2

The main city library is just north of the city centre. Designed by architect Erik Gunnar Asplund and sporting a curvaceous, technicolour reading room, it's the finest example of Stockholm's 1920s neoclassicist style. (📞08-50 83 10 60; Sveavägen 73; admission free; ⏱10am-7pm Mon-Fri, noon-4pm Sat; 🚇Odenplan)

Local Life
Park Life

Hang out in the amazing, multifaceted **Vasaparken**, a huge park that runs alongside Odengatan and has al fresco exercise options, a running track, football pitches, quiet places to read and a giant playground where kids can run wild.

Sven-Harrys Konstmuseum

MUSEUM

3 Map p114, B3

This ultramodern building houses an art gallery with interesting temporary exhibitions (recently a collection of August Strindberg's paintings, borrowed from Strindbergsmuseet, as well as a recreation of the former Lidingö home of owner and art collector Sven-Harry Karlsson. Access to the home is by guided tour (150kr, 45 minutes, currently in Swedish only). There's also an award-winning restaurant with terrace seating facing the park. (☑08-51 16 00 60; www.sven-harrys. se; Eastmansvägen 10-12; adult/child 100kr/ free; ☉11am-7pm Wed-Fri, to 5pm Sat & Sun; 🚇Odenplan)

Strindbergsmuseet

MUSEUM

4 Map p114, D4

The small but evocative Strindbergsmuseet in the Blue Tower is the well-preserved apartment where writer and painter August Strindberg (1849–1912) spent his final four years. Visitors can peep into his closet, scan his study and library (containing some 3000 volumes), do a round of the dining room and take in the often absorbing temporary exhibits. (☑08-411 53 54; www.strindbergsmuseet.se; Drottninggatan 85; adult/child 75/50kr; 🚇Rådmansgatan)

Eating

Caffè Nero

CAFE $$

5 Map p114, E2

Packed with local hipsters during the busy lunch hour, this stylish but casual neighbourhood cafe serves substantial Italian meals (fish, pasta, salads) at good prices, plus sublime coffee and pastries. Next door is a more formal bar-restaurant, Buco Nero, with DJs most nights. (www. nerostockholm.se; Roslagsgatan 4; lunch mains 110-145kr, dinner mains 145-175kr; ☉7am-4pm Mon-Fri, 9am-5pm Sat & Sun; 🚇Odenplan, Rådmansgatan)

Tranan

SWEDISH $$$

6 Map p114, C2

Locals pack this former beer hall, now a comfy but classy neighbourhood bistro with a seafood-heavy menu and chequered tablecloths. The food combines Swedish *husmanskost* (home cooking) with savvy Gallic touches; don't miss the fried herring. In summer, choose an outdoor table and watch the human dramas across Odenplan. On weekends, DJs and bands perform in the basement bar. (☑08-52 72 81 00; www.tranan.se; Karlbergsvägen 14; starters

35-285kr, mains 160-395kr; ⏰11.30am-11pm Mon-Fri, noon-11pm Sat & Sun, 5-11pm daily Jul & Aug; Odenplan)

Storstad FRENCH, SWEDISH $$$

7 Map p114, D2

This attractive bistro near Odenplan, which shares a corner (and owners) with Olssons bar (p119), serves Scandi classics like *toast skagen* or Swedish meatballs alongside traditional French favourites like *moules frites* and tarte Tatin. It transforms into a lively cocktail bar later in the evening. (www.storstad.se; Odengatan 41; plates 125-325kr; ⏰4pm-1am Mon-Wed, to 3am Fri & Sat; Odenplan)

Lao Wai VEGETARIAN $$$

8 Map p114, D3

Tiny, herbivorous Lao Wai does great things to tofu and vegetables, hence the faithful regulars. Everything here is gluten-free and vegan. A different Asian-fusion lunch special is served each weekday; the dinner menu is more expansive, offering virtuous treats like Sichuan-style smoked tofu with shiitake, chillies, garlic shoots, snow peas and black beans. (☑08-673 78 00; www.laowai.se; Luntmakargatan 74; dagens lunch 110kr, dinner mains 220-240kr; ⏰11am-2pm Mon-Fri, 5.30-9pm Mon-Sat; ; Rådmansgatan)

Vurma CAFE $$

9 Map p114, B3

This comfy cafe is part of a chainlet of restaurants and serves filling, healthy salads, soups, curries and sandwiches. (www.vurma.se; Gästrikegatan 2; mains 99-139kr; ⏰11am-8pm; ; St Eriksplan)

Konditori Ritorno CAFE $

10 Map p114, B3

The cosy backroom at this unpresumptuous cafe looks like the lobby of an old movie house fallen on hard times. A hit with writers, students and pensioners, its worn leather couches and miniature jukeboxes at every table make it a perfect pit stop for old-school shrimp sandwiches and heavenly *semla* buns. (☑08-32 01 06; Odengatan 80-82; sandwiches from 50kr; ⏰7am-10pm Mon-Thu, to 8pm Fri, 8am-6pm Sat, 10am-6pm Sun; Odenplan)

Flippin' Burgers BURGERS $$

11 Map p114, C3

Part of Stockholm's current obsession with burgers, Flippin' Burgers has a brief menu (just a few types of burger, fries and shakes) and a perpetual line

Top Tip

Affordable Fine Dining

At high-end restaurants you can sample fine dining on a more reasonable budget by ordering the daily lunch special, wherever you decide to eat – it's usually a great choice anyway, but also comes with salad, bread and coffee.

Understand

Eating in Stockholm

Sweden has come a long way from the days of all-beige fish and potato platters. Not only has immigration and membership in the EU introduced new flavours to the Swedish menu, a new wave of bold young chefs has been experimenting with traditional Swedish fare and melding it with various other influences. The result is an exciting dining scene on a par with some of the best food cities in Europe.

Classic Cuisine

Traditional Swedish cuisine is based on simple, everyday ingredients known generally as *husmanskost,* or basic home cooking. The most famous example of this, naturally, is Swedish meatballs. Other classic *husmanskost* dishes, largely based around fish and potatoes, include various forms of pickled and fried herring, cured salmon (gravlax) and *pytt i panna,* a potato hash served with sliced beets and a fried egg on top that may be the ultimate comfort food. Open-face shrimp sandwiches are everywhere, piled high with varying degrees of art and mayonnaise. Of course, the most thorough introduction to all the staples of Swedish cooking is the smörgåsbord, commonly available during the winter holidays.

Modern Menus

Essentially, contemporary Swedish cuisine melds global influences with local produce and innovation. Locals have rediscovered the virtues of their own pantry, alongside the more intense flavours arriving in Sweden from abroad. The result is a great passion for seasonal, home-grown ingredients, whether apples from Kivik or bleak roe from Kalix, used in creative new ways. Equally important is the seasonality of food: expect succulent berries in spring, artichokes and crayfish in summer, and hearty truffles and root vegetables in the colder months. Alongside this appreciation for the cycles of farming has come a newfound reliance on sustainable, small-scale farmers and organic produce. Increasingly, restaurants and cafes pride themselves on serving organically grown and raised food, as well as actively supporting ethical, eco-friendly agricultural practices.

Local Life
Who's for a Beer?

There are plenty of casual neighbourhood pubs and corner bars around Vasastan. The pick of the bunch is probably **Tennstopet** (Map p114, C3; ☎ 08-32 25 18; www. tennstopet.se; Dalagatan 50; dagens 129kr; ⏱ 11.30am-1am Mon-Fri, 1pm-1am Sat & Sun; 🚇 Odenplan); had there been a Swedish version of *Cheers*, it would've been filmed here. As much a place to eat as it is to drink, this atmospheric local haunt is festooned with oil paintings and gilded mirrors, winter candlelight setting the scene for a loveable cast of wizened regulars, corner-seat scribes and melancholy dames. Watch the show with a soothing *öl* (beer) and a serving of soulful *husmanskost*. Try the traditional herring platter for two (196kr).

out the front door. But things move quickly; squeeze into the bar for a Sam Adams while you wait. Burgers are simple and delicious, relying on high-quality ingredients (sustainably raised beef, ground in-house daily). (☎ 08-30 62 40; http://flippinburgers.se/en/; Observatoriegatan 8; burger 95-130kr, fries 35kr; ⏱ 4-10pm Mon-Thu, 11am-10pm Fri, noon-10pm Sat & Sun; 🚇 Odenplan)

Drinking

Olssons skor   BAR

12   🍺   Map p114, D2

The blue neon sign outside this bar tips you off to its former life as a shoe store. These days, it serves as the back bar to Storstad (p117), forming a busy corner of activity along this neighbourhoody street. (☎ 08-673 38 00; Odengatan 41; ⏱ 9pm-3am Wed-Sat; 🚇 Odenplan)

Shopping

Cajsa Warg   FOOD

13   🔒   Map p114, A3

A gourmet food store that focuses on sustainable products and a tranquil, pleasant shopping atmosphere, Cajsa Warg is fun to browse but also makes for a mean picnic basket if you're so inclined. Pick up gift boxes and souvenir treats to take home. (☎ 08-33 01 20; www.cajsawarg.se; St Eriksplan 2; ⏱ 8am-8pm Mon-Fri, 10am-7pm Sat & Sun, open later in summer; 🚇 St Eriksplan)

Top Sights
Stockholm Archipelago

Getting There

The archipelago's gateway is road-accessible Vaxholm, 35km northeast of Stockholm.

♆ Waxholmsbolaget (www.waxholmsbola get.se) is the main operator; single trips cost 47–130kr

Mention the archipelago to Stockholmers and prepare for gushing adulation. Buffering the city from the open Baltic Sea to the east, it's a mesmerising wonderland of rocky isles carpeted with deep forests and fields of wildflowers, dotted with yachts and little red wooden cottages.

Exactly how many islands there are is debatable, with headcounts ranging from 14,000 to 100,000 (the general consensus is 24,000). It's an unmissable area and much closer to the city than many visitors imagine, with regular ferry services and various organised tours.

Boathouse, Arholma (p122)

Vaxholm

There are plenty of reasons to visit Vaxholm, the most obvious being that it is the closest archipelago island to Stockholm (there's even a bridge – you can catch a bus here). The island offers a charming taster of this extraordinarily diverse area; on a sunny spring day, its crooked streets and storybook houses are irresistible. **Hembygdsgård** (☑08-54 13 19 80; Trädgårdsgatan 19; admission free; ◷11am-5pm May–mid-Sep) is a museum preserving some of these fine old homes. Vaxholm has a thriving restaurant scene, including the landmark Waxholms Hotell. For baked goodies, try **Boulangerie Cafe** (☑08-54 13 18 72; South Port 6; snacks from 75kr; ◷6.30am-6.30pm Mon-Thu, to 7pm Fri, 8am-7pm Sat). There's a helpful **tourist office** (☑08-54 13 14 80; www.vaxholmdestination.se; Rådhuset; ◷10am-6pm Mon-Fri, to 4pm Sat & Sun May-Aug, shorter hr rest of year) here, too.

Utö

Star of the archipelago's southern section, Utö has it all: sublime sandy beaches; lush forests; sleepy farms; abundant birdlife; an awesome organic bakery, **Utö Bageri** (Gruvbryggan; breakfast 85-145kr, lunch from 150kr, sandwiches 45-95kr; ◷8am-5pm); and a highly rated restaurant, **Nya Dannekrogen** (☑08-50 15 70 79; www.nyadannekrogen.se; Bygatan 1; mains 180-295kr, pizzas from 135kr; ◷May-Sep). Utö's network of level roads and trails make for heavenly cycling sessions; ask at the **tourist office** (☑08-50 15 74 10; www.uto.se/en/uto-tourist-office; Gruvbryggan; ◷10am-6pm May-Sep) about cycle hire. The best sandy beach is **Stora Sand** on the south coast. Gruvbryggan, the island's northernmost village, is the main ferry stop. **Utö Vårdshus** (☑08-50 42 03 00; www.utovardshus.se; Gruvbryggan; r hostel/hotel from 690/1600kr) is the island's only hotel/hostel.

☑ **Top Tips**

▸ Waxholmsbolaget divides the archipelago into three sections: middle, north and south. Within each section, several numbered routes go out and back, usually once a day, calling at various ports along the way.

▸ Keep in mind that most island villages are remote, with limited options for dining and groceries; bring some provisions along. There are also bar-restaurants on the boats.

✗ **Take a Break**

You're likely to end up in Vaxholm on any archipelago journey, either to change ferries or just strolling around to enjoy the pretty harbour town. While you're here, head to the historic **Waxholms Hotell** (☑08-54 13 01 50; www.waxholms hotell.se; Hamngatan 2; buffet 395kr, mains 169-305kr; ◷noon-10.30pm Mon-Sat, to 9pm Sun) for a scrumptious seafood meal.

Understand

Fast or Slow?

There are essentially two ways to visit the archipelago, depending on your preferred travel style.

If time is short, take an organised boat tour of anywhere from a few hours to a full day, passing several islands and making brief stops at one or two. Check with Stromma Kanalbolaget (p65) for options that suit you – the most thorough option is the popular 'Thousand Islands' day tour (from 1235kr), which includes lunch and dinner and takes in parts of the outer archipelago.

Otherwise, you can plan your own longer, slower, self-guided trip using **Waxholmsbolaget** (✆08-600 10 00; www.waxholmsbolaget.com/visitor; Strömkajen; 🕑7am-2pm Mon, 8am-2pm Tue-Thu, 7.30am-4.30pm Fri, 8am-noon Sat, 8.30am-noon Sun; Kungsträdgården) services with overnight stays. The area's many comfortable hostels, campsites and cushy hotels – plus some excellent restaurants – make the latter option dreamy if you have a few days to spare, though it does take a bit more planning.

Arholma

Arholma is a quiet, idyllic island in the archipelago's far north. Practically everything here was burnt down during a Russian invasion in 1719. The landmark lighthouse was rebuilt in the 19th century and is now an art gallery with impressive views. The entire island is a nature reserve, with hiking trails, cycle paths, kayaking routes, sandy beaches and even a forest zip line. The excellent **STF Arholma/Bull-August Gård** (✆0176-560 50; www.bullaugust.se; Arholma Södra Byväg 8; d from 650kr; 🅿📶) hostel is here, too.

Finnhamn

Actually a congregation of islands, Finnhamn combines lush woods and meadows with sheltered coves, rocky cliffs and visiting eagle owls. It's a popular summertime spot, but there are enough quiet corners to indulge your inner hermit. Walking trails cover the island, delivering some awesome views. You can rent kayaks, canoes and SUPs at the kiosk at Paradisviken, in the middle of the island. Don't miss the top-notch restaurant, **Finnhamns Café & Krog** (✆08-54 24 62 12; www.finnhamn.se; Ingmarsö; lunch mains 145-165kr, dinner mains 165-285kr; 🕑11.30am-9pm Fri & Sat, to 4.30pm Sun May & Sep), known for its regional specialities and seafood. **STF Vandrarhem Utsikten** (✆08-54 24 62 12; www.finnhamn.se; 2-/3-/4-bed r 820/1050/1250kr, 2-/4-bed cabins 820/890kr; 🕑year-round; @📶) is the island's hostel.

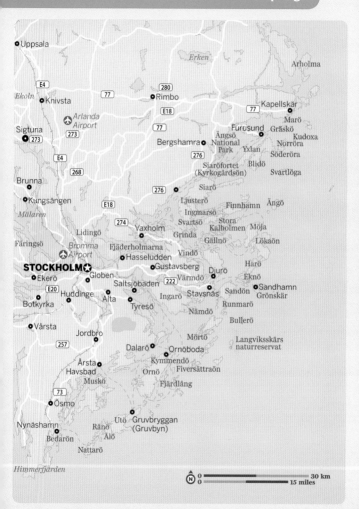

Uppsala

Erken

Arholma

Ecoln

E4

Knivsta

77

280

Rimbo

Kapellskär

E18

77

Marö

Sigtuna

273

Arlanda Airport

273

77

Furusund

Gräskö

Kudoxa

Ängsö National Park

Norröra

Bergshamra

276

Yxlan

Söderöra

E4

Siaröfortet (Kyrkogårdsön)

Blidö

268

Svartlöga

Brunna

Siarö

Kungsängen

276

Ljusterö

Finnhamn

Ängö

E18

Ingmarsö

Mälaren

274

Svartsö

Stora Kalholmen

Möja

Färingsö

Lidingö

Vaxholm

Grinda

Gällnö

Lökaön

Bromma Airport

Fjäderholmarna

Vindö

Harö

STOCKHOLM

Hasseludden

Gustavsberg

Diurö

Ekerö

Globen

Värmdö

Eknö

E20

Saltsjöbaden

222

Sandhamn

Huddinge

Ingarö

Stavsnäs

Sandön

Grönskär

Botkyrka

Alta

Tyresö

Runmarö

Nämdö

Bullerö

Vårsta

Jordbro

Mörtö

Langviksskärs naturreservat

257

Dalarö

Ornöboda

Årsta

Kymmendö

Havsbad

Ornö

Fiversättraön

Muskö

Fjärdlång

73

Ösmo

Nynäshamn

Rånö

Utö

Gruvbryggan (Gruvbyn)

Bedarön

Ålö

Nattarö

Himmerfjärden

0 — 30 km
0 — 15 miles

The Best of
Stockholm

Gamla Stan (p22)
SCANRAIL/GETTY IMAGES ©

Best Walks
Gamla Stan & Around

🏃 The Walk

Gamla Stan transports you back in time to Stockholm's early history. Most of the tourist activity is concentrated on Västerlånggatan and Stora Nygatan, but if you venture into the back alleys and quieter, more crooked streets, you'll find a city that seems almost unchanged since medieval times.

Start Gamla Stan

Finish Gamla Stan

Length 2.5km; 1½ hours

✗ Take a Break

Stop in at the casual **Cafe Järntorget** (Västerlånggatan 81; ice cream 1/2/3 scoops 40/50/60kr; ⏱8am-6pm Mon-Fri, 10am-6pm Sat & Sun, open late in summer; 🚇Gamla Stan) for a scoop or two (you'll want at least two) of the most eccentrically Swedish ice-cream flavours you'll ever find, from raspberry (*hallon*) with Turkish pepper to black liquorice.

VERONIKA GALKINA/SHUTTERSTOCK ©

Riddarholmskyrkan

❶ Riddarholmen

Other than its lovely **cathedral** (p30), this undervisited islet doesn't have a lot in the way of tourist activity, but it's extremely pretty to wander around, with its cobblestone streets and compressed huddle of fairy-tale buildings in delicate pastel shades.

❷ Evert Taubes Terrass

At the far west side of Riddarholmen is this flat terrace covered with tiny paving stones and decorated with impressive sculptures at either end. The singing lute player, *Everlife,* portrays the terrace's namesake, Swedish troubadour Evert Taube, in a 1990 bronze by Willy Gordon. The sculpture at the opposite end is *Solbåten* (1966), by Christian Berg.

❸ Riddarhuset

Heading back towards Gamla Stan, you'll pass Riddarhuset, a big pink-and-turquoise building that slightly resembles a wedding cake. This is the House of Nobility (or House of Knights), designed by French father–son architects

Simon and Jean de la Vallée and completed in 1660. The statue in front is Axel Oxenstierna (1583–1654), a close adviser to Queen Christina.

❹ Stortorget

Make your way to Mynttorget and turn down Västerlånggatan, the main shopping street, for a few blocks, then zigzag up to quieter Prästgatan. Turn left up the hill to Stortorget, the old town's beautiful main square. It's lined with gorgeous old buildings and usually

filled with happy holidaymakers; you'd never know it was once the scene of a massacre (the Stockholm Bloodbath of 1520).

❺ Köpmantorget

Stroll down Köpmangatan ('Merchant's Street') to the triangular 'square' at its end, where you'll find a 1912 bronze replica of Berndt Notke's wooden statue from the 1400s, *St George and the Dragon,* which occupies **Storkyrkan** (p32). Take the road that slopes off to the right, and

continue along Österlånggatan, another major commercial thoroughfare.

❻ Järntorget

At the end of Österlånggatan is this pretty square, barely younger than Stortorget (it dates to 1300). It began as an important trade spot, first for corn, then iron. As you continue back towards the starting point, peek up Mårten Trötzigs gränd – the narrowest street in town, which squiggles off to the right from Västerlånggatan.

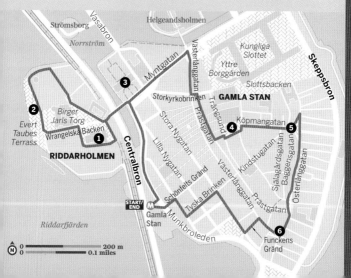

Best Walks
Water's Edge Walk

🏃 The Walk

It's not for nothing Stockholm calls itself 'Beauty on Water'. The city is built across 14 islands and has miles of waterfront. This walk takes you along some of the best bits, with maximum postcard potential and a few key places to stop. It's best to do it in the late afternoon or early evening, and don't forget to bring a camera.

Start Slussen

Finish Nybrokajen

Length 8km; one to three hours

🍴 Take a Break

For a quick snack that couldn't possibly be more typically Swedish, grab a herring plate from the **Nystekt Strömming** (p77) cart outside the Slussen tunnelbana stop. There's a picnic table nearby for resting your legs.

Strömparterren

ROLF G WACKENBERG/SHUTTERSTOCK ©

❶ Monteliusvägen

Follow Hornsgatan west from the Slussen tunnelbana stop; you'll pass **Akkurat** (p79), noteworthy as an excellent place to find good beer in Stockholm. Turn right at Bellmansgatan, then left at Bastugatan, which leads you to the tiny footpath called Monteliusvägen. This path extends through historic houses on one side, and on the other offers amazing views across the water and over the town.

❷ Fjällgatan

Cross back over the Slussen area and take Katarinavägen up the hillside, until it connects with Fjällgatan. This tiny street is the twin of Monteliusvägen – a gravel track through antique houses, it provides astounding views over the city from a slightly different angle. At its start/end point near **Hermans Trädgårdscafé** (p76) there's a rickety set of stairs leading down to the ground-level street, Stadsgårdsleden. Follow this back towards Slussen.

❸ Skeppsbrokajen

Stay next to the water as you walk across Gamla Stan, following Skeppsbron and Skeppsbrokajen. You'll see lots of boat traffic through here, and there's an uninterrupted view across the water (Strömmen) of Skeppsholmen.

❹ Strömparterren

Round the corner by the **palace** (p24) and turn right to walk across Norrbro. This small bridge, which crosses the sculpted park area known as Strömparterren, was nearly demolished to make way for a parking lot. Instead, thanks to some important underground discoveries, it now houses the excellent **Medeltidsmuseet** (p30). Follow the bridge and turn right, keeping to the water's edge as you walk alongside Norrström and onto the footbridge to Skeppsholmen.

❺ Kastellet

Walk along the westernmost edge of the parklike Skeppsholmen, passing by the famous floating youth hostel **Vandrarhem af Chapman & Skeppsholmen**. At the far end of the island is an even smaller islet, called Kastellholmen, where there's a fortress called Kastellet. Circle the edge of the islet for what is essentially a 360-degree, panoramic view of the surrounding areas, including Gamla Stan, Södermalm and Djurgården.

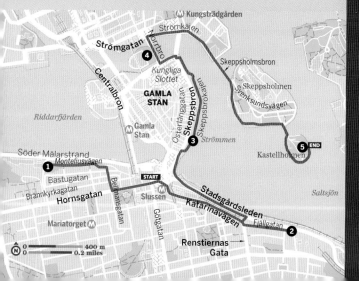

Best
Eating

Stockholm is a city of food obsessions. The relatively small city has more than half a dozen Michelin-starred restaurants, with new and exciting places opening constantly, serving everything from veggie-minded superfoods to fast-food fads like the indefatigable burger. It's not unusual for people to plan their visits here around restaurant menus.

LEISA TYLER/LIGHTROCKET VIA GETTY IMAGES ©

Daily Dining

If you don't plan on daily five-star dining, Stockholm's cafes offer a good range of standard fare (salads, sandwiches, quiche). Vegetarians and the health-conscious are in luck, too, thanks to the recent explosion of 'green' restaurants serving nourishing superfood bowls of fresh produce and grains. At the other end of the spectrum, the city is currently obsessed with cheeseburgers.

Street Snacks

In Swedish street food, hot dogs reign supreme – the basic model is called a *grillad korvmed bröd* (hot dog in a bun), although you can also ask for it boiled (*kokt*). Adventurous souls can request myriad different things done to their *korv*, chiefly involving rolling it up in flatbread with accompaniments from shrimp salad to mashed potatoes.

Festive Flavours

Around Christmas, many restaurants offer a *julbord,* a particularly gluttonous version of Sweden's world-famous smörgåsbord buffet. Among the usual delicacies of herring, gravlax, meatballs, short ribs and blood pudding are seasonal gems like *Janssons frestelse,* a casserole of sweet cream, potato, onion and anchovy.

☑ **Top Tips**

▶ The weekday lunch special called *dagens rätt* is great value (90kr to 130kr). It's a set menu served between 11am and 2pm, including a hot main dish, salad, drink, bread and coffee.

▶ Many vegetarian eateries are also all-you-can-eat buffets, which are massively popular with locals.

▶ For Swedish *husmanskost* (home cooking: meatballs, fried herring, etc), head to old-school pubs and traditional restaurants.

Best Restaurants

Kryp In An intimate, excellent dining spot in Gamla Stan, which manages to be upmarket without pretension. (p32)

Rosendals Trädgård-skafe Enjoy gorgeous produce in the midst of Djurgården botanical splendour. (p66)

Hermans Trädgårdscafé A top-flight vegetarian buffet with wide-open Södermalm views. (p76)

Grands Verandan Best place in town to launch into a classic Swedish smörgåsbord. In Norrmalm. (p45)

Woodstockholm New twists on traditional Swedish dishes. There's a wine bar here, too. (p76)

Ekstedt Reindeer and pike-perch cooked in a wood-fired oven – what's not to like? (p90; pictured left)

Best Vegetarian

Hermitage A fantastic veggie buffet in Gamla Stan. (p32)

Holy Greens A super-healthy take on fast food in Norrmalm: various delicious bowls of super-foods and proteins. (p45)

Mahalo Healthy bowls of greens, grains and trendy good-for-you things. In Södermalm. (p78)

Chutney Heaping plates of vegetarian curries and stews in Södermalm. (p76)

Rutabaga Artful veggie delights from celebrity chef Mathias Dahlgren. (p43)

Best Traditional Swedish

Magnus Ladulås Swedish classics served in a medieval Gamla Stan setting. (p34)

Fem Små Hus A perfect combination of authentic historical setting and traditional cuisine. (p34)

Pelikan An old-school Swedish beer hall with a solid menu of classics. If you haven't tried herring or reindeer here, here's your chance. (p77)

Sturekatten Sip coffee or tea with cakes at this adorable old-school Östermalm cafe. (p92)

Best
Cafes

Cafes and coffee are integral to Swedish life, to the point that meeting friends for a coffee break has its own verb: *fika*. Swedes drink more coffee than people in any other country except Finland (something to do with the weather?). The range of coffee drinks has vastly increased in recent years, as has the variety of places to enjoy them. Don't forget to include a sweet – Stockholm's cafes do seriously good cakes and pastries.

JULIE MAYFENG/SHUTTERSTOCK ©

Best Coffee Shops

Sturekatten Cute labyrinthine coffee shop with antique furniture and delicious cakes. In Östermalm. All very dignified. (p92)

Bianchi Cafe & Cycles Perfect espresso in a bicycle-themed Italian cafe in Norrmalm. Saddle up. (p39)

Café Saturnus Surely the largest cinnamon buns in all of Stockholm (and probably the best mosaic floor) are to be found in Östermalm. (p91)

Wiener Caféet A gorgeous Norrmalm art-deco space serving excellent food. Come for afternoon high tea with killer cakes. (p45)

String Homey neighbourhood corner cafe in Södermalm, with a great weekend breakfast buffet. The house-made hummus takes the cake. (p77)

Rosendals Trädgårdskafe Pastries, impressive organic salads and coffee in botanical garden surrounds – feel like you're on holiday now? (p66)

Grillska Husets Konditori Awesome bakery with outdoor seating on Gamla Stan's historic main square. Don't bypass the shrimp sandwich. (p34)

☑ Top Tip

▶ For Stockholmers, coffee isn't just a breakfast kick-starter. The caffeine flows freely here at any tick of the clock: locals are just as likely to enjoy a cup of the black stuff at 10pm as they are a beer.

Chokladkoppen Could this be Stockholm's favourite cafe? Another main-square stalwart in Gamla Stan. Mind your head. (p32)

Caffé Nero Almost aggressively cool Vasastan coffee shop serving substantial Italian meals. Hit the bar next door after dark. (p116)

Best
Museums &
Galleries

JO CREBBIN/SHUTTERSTOCK ©

Stockholm does museums properly – there's really not a bad one in the bunch. Maybe it's a perk of having a design-obsessed culture – whatever the reason, this city makes learning fun. Its art galleries are intensely stylish, the kind of places you want to dress up for, and its history museums employ multimedia to engage and enthral you (and the kids).

Best Museums

Kungliga Slottet The royal palace contains a number of museums and is itself a masterpiece – it's the world's largest royal castle, still used for its original purpose. (p24)

Skansen An open-air museum of Swedish history and culture. Plan on spending at least a day exploring. (p52, pictured above right)

Vasamuseet Purpose-built museum devoted to the story of the ill-fated warship *Vasa*, which sank to the bottom of the sea in 1628. (p56)

Historiska Museet Engrossing multimedia presentation of the country's culture and history,

arcing across 10,000 years. (p84)

Nobelmuseet Be inspired by stories of the most creative people of our time – recipients of the Nobel Prize. (p30)

Medeltidsmuseet Take the kids on a time-travelling tour of medieval Stockholm and the underpinnings of the royal palace. (p30)

Nordiska Museet Swedish art and artefacts through the ages, entertainingly arranged. (p63)

Spritmuseum A fun look at the complicated relationship Sweden has with alcohol. And there are tastings! (p63)

Tekniska Museet Kids of all ages will be fascinated by seeing how stuff works. Interactivity is the

name of the game: push, pull, prod, measure and test. (p97)

Nationalmuseum It's big! The nation's largest collection of arts, across the ages. (p42)

Best Galleries

Moderna Museet One of the best places in Europe to check out some astounding modern art. (p58)

Fotografiska Go snap-happy at this stylish Södermalm photographic museum/gallery. (p70)

Bonniers Konsthall Cutting-edge art in a cutting-edge building in Vasastan. (p115)

Prins Eugens Waldemarsudde An excellent Nordic art gallery in a beautiful waterside location. (p65)

Best
Nightlife

Nightlife in Stockholm ranges from a quiet pint in an underground cellar to a neon-lit club that only gets kicking around 3am. If you're just aiming to grab a beer in a pub, even a nice one, no special arrangements are required. But if you plan to hit the late-night clubs, some preparation is required. If possible, check the website to see if you can slip your name onto the guest list – this is especially useful if you're on a tight schedule or only have one night to go clubbing and don't want to risk being shut out. Dress to the nines and follow your instincts – or follow the crowd – and you're bound to find a good time.

LOOK DIE BILDAGENTUR DER FOTOGRAFEN GMBH/ ALAMY STOCK PHOTO ©

☑ Top Tips

▶ Coat checks are mandatory in many clubs and bars. There's usually a small fee (20kr to 30kr).

▶ On popular nights, clubs may also charge a fairly hefty admission fee (150kr to 200kr) – and make you wait in line (unless you've managed to get yourself on the guest list).

▶ Some clubs stay open later than the tunnelbana runs. Budget for a taxi.

Best Clubs & Bars

Akkurat A great Södermalm beer bar, with mussels on the menu. (p79)

Berns Salonger Fancy, well-designed space with loads of history. Live music and DJs. (p46)

Café Opera Rock stars cavort in one of the loveliest interiors in Stockholm. (p46; pictured above right)

East Good sushi and great cocktails at this Stureplan hang-out. (p46)

Kvarnen Traditional Södermalm beer hall with a popular late-night dance space. (p78)

Sturecompagniet The relatively low-key option in Stureplan, in a pretty, baroque space. (p92)

Lemon Bar Friendly Kungsholmen cocktail bar where late-night dancing is a very real possibility. (p104)

Solidaritet A Norrmalm dance club hosting electronic music and international DJs. (p46)

Debaser Strand Cool, friendly Södermalm bar with regular live music, at Hornstull beach. (p79)

Spy Bar A famously difficult club to get into, unless you're famous (or at least look like you are). (p92)

Best
Live Music

Stockholm's music scene is alive and kicking. On any night you can catch emerging indie acts, edgy rock, blues and Balkan pop. Jazz has a particularly strong presence, with several legendary venues saxing it up and an annual jazz festival in October. Classical concerts can be surprisingly affordable, and big names in rock and pop music tour through the city regularly.

LONELY PLANET/GETTY IMAGES ©

Jazz

Swedish jazz has been going strong since the 1930s, and peaked in the '50s with artists such as Lars Gullin and Monica Zetterlund. Live jazz clubs are popular; the annual Stockholm Jazz Festival (p144) is mandatory listening.

Rock & Pop

Everyone knows about ABBA of course, and fans can check out their museum (p64)...but there's a lot more to Swedish pop than Agnetha, Björn, Benny and Frida. Sweden is the third-largest exporter of music in the world, behind the US and UK, remarkable when you consider the size of the population.

Opera & Classical

There's no shortage of live experiences in the classical or operatic realms here, either. The Stockholm opera house is a national landmark, while the classical Konserthuset is both affordable and accessible.

Best Jazz & Rock

Glenn Miller Café Jazz and blues bar with a devoted crowd of Norrmalm regulars. (p48)

Debaser Strand Indie rock and mainstream live acts. (p79)

Mosebacke Etablissement Big-name live bands and local faves hit this Södermalm stage. (p80)

Stampen Homey jazz and blues joint in Gamla Stan. (p34)

Fasching The premier jazz club in Stockholm, with weekend DJs. (p48; pictured above)

Best Opera & Classical

Konserthuset Classical concerts are held in this elegant blue building in Norrmalm. (p48)

Operan The royal opera house is in Norrmalm – any visit here is an experience. (p48)

Best
Shopping

Shopping is a sport, a pleasure and an art form in Stockholm – a seasoned shopper's paradise. Whether you're just browsing or looking for specific gifts to bring home, there are plenty of options spread across the various neighbourhoods. Even when it's cold and dark outside, the city's terrific malls and department stores don't miss a commercial beat.

STEFAN HOLM/SHUTTERSTOCK ©

What to Buy

Quintessentially Swedish things to bring home as gifts and souvenirs include hand-carved wooden toys and figures, such as the famous painted Dalahäst figures; glass and crystal, both decorative and utilitarian; fine linens and textiles; and intricate Sami handicrafts, especially leather, woodwork and jewellery made of woven metal threads.

Where to Shop

For big-name Swedish and international retail outlets and high-end boutiques, hit the pedestrianised Biblioteksgatan from Östermalm to Norrmalmstorg, as well as the smaller streets that branch off it.

For funkier, artier and secondhand stores and galleries, head to Södermalm. And for classic souvenirs, T-shirts and postcards, check out picturesque Gamla Stan.

☑ Top Tip

On most major purchases, depending on where you live, you can reclaim your sales tax at customs when departing Sweden. Keep your receipts and ask for a tax-free form from the vendor.

Best Malls & Department Stores

NK Huge department store in Norrmalm with upscale souvenirs and household goods. (p49; pictured above right)

Åhléns Excellent department store with a great range of items and multiple locations. (p49)

Gallerian A central shopping mall near Sergels Torg in Norrmalm. (p49)

Mood Stockholm Hip, stylish shopping centre in Norrmalm. (p49)

Västermalmsgallerian Busy mall right outside the Fridhemsplan tunnelbana stop. (p107)

PK Huset A very central shopping mall, big on Swedish brands. (p49)

Best
Fashion

Stockholm is Sweden's (and as the experts attest, Scandinavia's) fashion hub, and a major producer and exporter of emerging design talent. The big shopping districts are also home to just about every imaginable international design name, from Stella McCartney to Louis Vuitton. There are also fabulous secondhand and vintage shops across the city (sometimes being progressive means looking back).

CHRISTIAN VIERIG/GETTY IMAGES ©

Sustainability

Perhaps unsurprisingly in a country as green as Sweden, sustainability is a big issue in fashion (historically, the industry has had its failings). Several Swedish brands place an emphasis on keeping their manufacturing processes eco-friendly and ethical. Check out the **Sustainable Fashion Academy** (www.sustainablefashionacademy.org) for more.

Best Contemporary Fashion

Acne Skinny jeans and impeccable cool, now world-famous and highly sought-after. (p38)

Marimekko Wild, playful patterns on everything from frocks to handbags and kitchen gadgets. (p38)

Filippa K Dead-serious design for grown-ups (also possibly the inventor of skinny jeans). (p39)

Whyred Understated and street-smart clothing inspired by musicians. (p39)

BLK DNM A new venture from the sketchbook of J Lindeberg. (p39)

WESC Skater-inspired fashion and gear, marketed worldwide by the rich and famous. (p39)

Best Vintage

59 Vintage Store High-quality retro clothing

from the '50s through '70s. (p104)

Judits Famously well-curated vintage clothing. (p81)

Lisa Larsson Second Hand Cool secondhand clothes in a fun shop. (p80)

Smiley Vintage Remade styles from vintage clothing. (p81)

Best
Design

Scandinavia is famous for ahead-of-its-time design, and there's plenty to be found around Stockholm. The city is all about good design, merging form and function in a relatively democratic – or at least ubiquitous – way. Bring samples of it back home with you, be inspired by how it's used, or just admire Scandistyle in its native environment.

Best Design

Svenskt Tenn The Josef Frank–led school of design still holds sway over the city. (p93)

Nordiska Galleriet A store that doubles as a showroom and design-freak nirvana. A dizzying array of nifty things. (p93)

Iris Hantverk Clever and beautifully made household items. (p39)

Nationalmuseum The largest collection of Swedish design objects can be found at the national art gallery. (p42)

Filippa K One of Sweden's groundbreaking early designers has shops in several locations around town. (p39)

DesignTorget This chain of accessible but cutting-edge design (household goods, gadgets etc) has several central locations. (p81)

Studio Lena M A cute little shop and studio featuring distinctive (and adorable) graphic designs, prints and textiles. (p35)

NK This department store has a fantastic selection of quintessentially Swedish design products, from serving trays to tea towels and candle holders. (p49)

E Torndahl Family-run Gamla Stan shop offering classic Swedish textiles and household items. (p35)

Marimekko Finnish design known for bold

☑ Top Tip

▶ For a new-design twist on the traditional Swedish wooden horses (Dalahäst), look into the work of Kerstin Oldal (www.kerstinoldal.com), who reinterprets the national symbol in gorgeous ways.

prints on textiles and dishes. (p38)

Café Opera Join the jet-set at this glitzy Norrmalm venue, revamped by Thomas Sandell. (p46)

Sturehof Popular high-end seafood restaurant and bar in Östermalm, designed by Jonas Bohlin. (p91; pictured above)

Best
With Kids

Stockholm is well set up for travelling with children. There are baby-changing tables in almost every public bathroom, and even top-end restaurants have high chairs and children's menus. Likewise, hotel and hostel staff are accustomed to catering to families, while public transportation is generally easy to navigate. On top of that, many museums offer free admission to children under 18 (sometimes older).

ROBERTO LA ROSA/SHUTTERSTOCK ©

☑ Top Tip

▶ Even if they aren't particularly geared towards children, most of Stockholm's museums have family playrooms available.

Best Kid-Friendly Sights

Junibacken Draws young readers into Swedish author Astrid Lindgren's fantastic world, home to Pippi Longstocking and her friends.

Naturhistoriska Riksmuseet Offers an interactive child's-eye view of the natural world (stuffed things, preserved things, exhumed things), with an entire section for hands-on science experiments. (p90)

Medeltidsmuseet Provides multimedia displays that transport visitors back in time to the city's earliest days. Under a bridge in Gamla Stan. (p30)

Gröna Lund Tivoli It's cheesy, but the carnival-ride entertainment here is always a hit with slightly older kids and teens. (p66)

Tekniska Museet Interactive science exhibits will entertain inquisitive brains for hours. (p97)

Skansen Essentially a younger child's paradise, with dozens of mini exhibits to explore, snacks everywhere, a zoo (pictured above right), singalongs and guides in old-timey costumes. (p52)

Nobelmuseet Has a 'Children's Club' (Barnens Nobelklubb) where kids aged between seven and 10 can share ideas and create. (p30)

Aquaria Vattenmuseum Though it has an educational message, this place is also just fun to wander through. Fish-feeding sessions are frenzied. (p64)

Best
For Free

S-F/SHUTTERSTOCK ©

Short on cash? Check museum schedules for free nights – most of them have one or two per week. Several museums also offer free admission to children (usually meaning anyone under age 18, sometimes up to 20). Public parks and beaches are a handy way to fill a budget afternoon, as is window-shopping in Norrmalm, people-watching in Södermalm or wandering through park-studded neighbourhoods like Djurgården or Gärdet.

Best Free Stuff

Stadshuset Swimming at City Hall is free, if you've got the gumption to dive from the terrace with the locals. (p100)

Rålambshovsparken Swim, play, picnic or just hang out with an airport novel in this large park in Kungsholmen. (p103)

Moderna Museet Free admission! Modern art! It's a winning combination and Stockholm's most challenging art museum. (p58)

Stampen Every Sunday afternoon around 2pm, the regular Stampen crowd gets busy with a blues jam. (p34)

Tekniska Museet From 5pm to 8pm Wednesday, bring the whole family

in to roam this huge, fun technology museum for free. (p97)

Kulturhuset There are plenty of free kids' activities at this arts hub, from hands-on crafts to a comic-book library. (p42)

Riksdagshuset Take an engaging free tour of the Swedish Parliament building in Gamla Stan. (p31; pictured above right)

Royal Armoury Check out the amazing old suits of armour and sundry scary weapons beneath the Royal Palace. (p30)

Medeltidsmuseet Delve into medieval Stockholm at this free museum, beneath a bridge between Norrmalm and Gamla Stan. (p30)

Mårten Trotzigs Gränd It won't cost you one red cent to traverse Stockholm's skinniest street. (p31)

Hallwylska Museet Who said hoarding was a bad thing? This amazing museum in Norrmalm offers a window into a *serious* collector's soul. (p42)

Armémuseum If you need convincing that war isn't the best way for people to spend their time, this free Östermalm museum will do the trick. (p90)

Sergels Torg Hang out in Norrmalm's hyperactive central square and watch the hum of humanity (...actually, it's more circular than square). (p43)

Best
LGBT

Stockholm is a dazzling spot for queer travellers. Sweden's legendary open-mindedness makes homophobic attitudes rare, and party-goers of all persuasions are welcome in any bar or club. As a result, Stockholm doesn't really have a gay district, although you'll find most of the queer-centric venues in Södermalm and Gamla Stan.

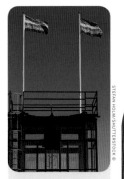

STEFAN HOLM/SHUTTERSTOCK ©

Best Bars & Clubs

Lady Patricia (☎08-743 05 70; www.patricia.st; Söder Mälarstrand, Kajplats 19; ☺5pm-midnight Wed & Thu, to 5am Fri-Sun; ㉇Slussen) Half-price seafood, nonstop dance music and decks packed with sexy Swedes and drag queens make this former royal yacht a gay Sunday night ritual (though you can now visit five nights a week). Head to the upper dance floor (past the pirates in the riggings) where lager-happy punters sing along to Swedish Eurovision entries with a bemusing lack of irony.

Side Track (☎08-641 16 88; www.sidetrack. nu; Wollmar Yxkullsgatan 7; ☺6pm-1am Wed-Sat; ㉇Mariatorget) Claiming the title of Stockholm's

oldest gay bar, this establishment in Södermalm has a low-key, publike ambience and decent bar food (fish and chips, curry, quesadillas). Check online for a schedule of theme nights and events.

Torget (☎08-20 55 60; www.torgetbaren.com; Mälartorget 13; ☺5pm-1am; ㉇Gamla Stan) For camp and Campari, it's hard to beat this sparkling gay bar – think rotating chandeliers, mock-baroque touches and different themed evenings, from live burlesque to handbag-swinging schlager. The crowd is a good source of info on upcoming underground parties, so grab a champers and chat away.

Best
Architecture

Stockholm has a well-preserved cache of buildings from various important eras of architecture. For a good overview of Swedish architecture and its various lineages, as well as quick primers on current movements, stop in at ArkDes (p66), right next door to Moderna Museet. And don't miss Globen (aka the Ericsson Globe; www.stockholmlive.com), the kooky giant golf-ball entertainment venue south of Södermalm.

JOHN COPLAND/SHUTTERSTOCK ©

Early Styles

Most of Stockholm's notable buildings are premodernist – the two royal palaces, Kungliga Slottet and Drottningholm, for example, and the imposing Stadshuset. A fairly brief but noteworthy period in regional architecture was Swedish National Romanticism – an often decorative classical free-style with Arts and Crafts influences, also known as Jugendstil.

Names to Drop

Erik Gunnar Asplund (1885–1940) is arguably Sweden's most important modern architect. He's responsible for the iconic Stadsbiblioteket as well as the stunning Skogskyrkogården cemetery. Another name you'll hear frequently is Peter Celsing, who designed the stubbornly contemporary Kulturhuset. Many of the most important buildings in Stockholm were designed by the court architect Nicodemus Tessin the Elder. Tessin the Younger designed the 'new' Kungliga Slottet and worked on several other standout buildings.

Best Buildings

Stadsbiblioteket A graceful building, anyway you look at it. (p115)

Kulturhuset The design of this 1974 arts centre pushes the envelope, and divides architectural tastes. (p42)

Dramaten The Royal Dramatic Theatre is a decadent example of Jugendstil glory. (p93; pictured above)

Stadshuset The City Hall is sturdy and square on the outside, secretly glittering within. (p100)

Östermalms Saluhall A many-spired cathedral of gourmet food, delectable both inside and out. (p90)

Best
Parks

Beautiful parks are a dime a dozen in Stockholm; you can hardly turn a corner without finding one. Most have good places for a picnic, shade trees, nice benches and sturdy playground equipment for kids. Some also have lakes or beaches for swimming, good hiking trails and sometimes even small cafes for refreshments. Make like the locals and enjoy!

Picnics

Many of Stockholm's casual cafes and coffee shops will offer breakfast or lunch 'packets', which make excellent-value picnic fixings. You can also pick up supplies in the prepared food section of many supermarkets, or in department stores such as NK (p49), whose high-end grocery section has the makings of a luxurious picnic.

Beaches

You're allowed to swim from just about any place in Stockholm where you can elbow your way into the water, but some swimming areas are nicer than others. Ask around – lots of locals have secret favourite beaches – or head to the Stockholm Archipelago or the water's edge near Rålambshovsparken.

Royal Parks

Some city parks have a royal lineage, notably Djurgården, both established and administered by various Swedish kings. They're now open to the public and are excellent places for running, walking or cycling (...don't worry, you're unlikely to encounter a deer-hunting king these days).

Best Parks

Djurgården The historical home of the royal game park, established in the 15th century (p60; pictured above).

Vasaparken Lovely oasis in the middle of Vasastan (p116).

Humlegården Home of the royal library in Östermalm, and a peaceful hang-out in its own right.

Rålambshovsparken This park abuts an excellent public swimming beach in Kungsholmen. (p103)

Ladugårdsgärdet Wide-open parklands just east of Östermalm (snooze away your jet lag).

Tantolunden Stay fit in Södermalm with an outdoor gym and waterside trails. (p76)

Best
Festivals & Events

There's nearly always something going on in Stockholm, especially during the summer months. Whether you're interested in grazing the offerings of some of the city's best restaurants, sampling some international music or film, or just exploring whatever's on the seasonal activity menu, you're likely to find something of interest. Ask what's on at the tourist office.

MATT MUNRO/LONELY PLANET ©

Best in Summer

Midsummer Arguably the most important Swedish holiday, Midsummer's Eve traditionally falls on the Friday between 19 and 25 June; revellers head to the countryside to raise the maypole (pictured above right), sing and dance, drink and eat pickled herring (Midsummer Day is usually spent recovering).

Smaka På Stockholm (A Taste of Stockholm; www. smakapastockholm.se; admission free; ⊙early Jun) A five-day celebration of Stockholm food. The program includes gourmet food stalls (including representatives from several archipelago restaurants), cooking demos and entertainment on Kungsträdgården. It's free to get in, and food offerings tend to be good value.

Stockholm Pride (www. stockholmpride.org/en; ⊙late Jul or early Aug) This annual parade and festival is dedicated to creating an atmosphere of freedom and support for gay, lesbian, bisexual and transgender people. It's one of the most exuberant pride festivals in Europe.

Best in Autumn & Winter

Stockholm Jazz Festival (www.stockholmjazz. com; varies by venue; ⊙Oct) One of Europe's premier jazz festivals happens every October.

Stockholm International Film Festival (www.stockholmfilmfestival. se; tickets 170kr; ⊙Nov) Screenings of new independent films, director talks and discussion panels draw cinephiles to this important festival; tickets go quickly, so book early if you're interested. The ticket office is in Kulturhuset.

Gamla Stan Christmas Market (www.stortor getsjulmarknad.com) Usually opening in mid-November, this adorable Stockholm market in Gamla Stan's main square (Stortorget) can almost single-handedly lift the spirits on a cold winter night. Shop for handicrafts and delicacies, or just wander with a mug of cocoa and a saffron bun.

Survival Guide

Survival Guide

Before You Go

When to Go

Stockholm

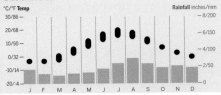

→ **Summer (mid-Jun–mid-Aug)** Stockholm's long days, uncannily pretty light and mild weather are dreamy.

→ **Winter (Dec–Feb)** The city is a frosted cake, with holiday markets and mugs of *glögg* around every corner.

→ **Autumn (Sep–Oct)** Cooler weather, minimal crowds and beautiful autumn colours.

Book Your Stay

→ Expect high-quality accommodation in Stockholm, although it can be expensive.

→ Rates are also much cheaper in summer and at weekends.

→ Svenska Turistföreningen (STF) hostels are affiliated with Hostelling International (HI).

Useful Websites

c/o Stockholm (www.costockholm.com) Booking service for rooms and B&Bs.

Lonely Planet (www.lonelyplanet.com/sweden/hotels) Recommendations and bookings.

Best Budget

Vandrarhem af Chapman & Skeppsholmen (www.stfchapman.com) Sleep on-board an antique ship at this popular hostel.

Långholmen Hotell & Vandrarhem (www.

langholmen.com) Spend the night in the most comfortable prison cell you're likely to come across.

City Backpackers (www.citybackpackers. org) A fun place and the most central hostel in Stockholm.

City Hostel (www. cityhostel.se) A quiet night's rest on a budget, in Kungsholmen.

Hostel Bed & Breakfast (www.hostelbedandbreak fast.com) Informal spot with good facilities.

Best Midrange

Hobo Hotel (www.hobo. se) Hipster and fun, in a fantastic central location.

Hotel 'C' Stockholm (www.nordicchotel.com) Design hotel with great location and breakfast.

Hotel Anno 1647 (www. rexhotel.se) A charming historic hotel near Slussen.

Birger Jarl Hotel (www. birgerjarl.se) One of the city's original design hotels.

Rex Hotel (www.rexhotel. se) Small but stylish rooms.

Best Top End

Grand Hôtel Stockholm (www.grandhotel.se) Iconic waterside luxury, where the glitterati stay.

Clarion Hotel Sign (www.clarionsign.com) Modern luxury hotel with cool design features.

Rival Hotel (www. rival.se) A retro boutique owned by one of the Bs from ABBA.

Hotel J (www.hotelj. com) This beautiful hotel makes it easy to pretend you own a yacht.

First Hotel Reisen (www. firsthotels.com) All the modern touches in an old town building.

Arriving in Stockholm

Stockholm Arlanda Airport

➜ **Arlanda Express** (www.arlandaexpress.com; Centralstation; one way adult/child 280/150kr, 2 adults one way in summer 350kr; 🚇 Centralen) trains between the airport and Centralstationen run every 10 to 15 minutes from 5am to

12.30am (less frequently after 9pm), taking 20 minutes.

➜ **Flygbussarna** (www. flygbussarna.se; Cityterminalen; 🚇 Centralen) buses to/from Cityterminalen leave from stop 11 in Terminal 5 every 10 to 15 minutes (adult/child one way 119/99kr, 40 minutes). Tickets can be purchased online, at Cityterminalen or at the Flygbuss self-service machine in Terminal 5.

➜ **Airport Cab** (🕾 08-25 25 25; www.airportcab.se),

Getting Around

Tunnelbana (Metro)

➜ Stockholm's underground train system connects its various neighbourhoods; it's fast and efficient.

➜ There are three main lines: green, red and blue. Route maps are easy to navigate and posted at all stations.

➜ Trains generally run from 5am to 2.30am, but check schedules online.

Bus

➜ Inner-city buses radiate from Sergels Torg, Odenplan, Fridhemsplan (on Kungsholmen) and **Slussen** (Map p74).

➜ Most run until midnight, but check schedules.

➜ Tickets cannot be bought on buses.

Bicycle

➜ Bicycles can be carried free on SL local trains as foldable 'hand luggage' only. They're not allowed in Centralstationen or on the tunnelbana.

➜ **Stockholm City Bikes** (www.citybikes.se; 3-day/ season card 165/300kr) has self-service bicycle-hire stands across the city. Bikes can be borrowed for three hours and returned at any City Bikes stand. Buy a bike card online or from the tourist office.

Taxi

➜ Taxis are readily available but fees are unregulated – check for a meter or arrange the fare first.

➜ Use one of the reputable firms, such as **Taxi Stockholm** (☏15 00 00; www.taxistockholm.se) or **Sverige Taxi** (☏020-20 20 20; www.sverigetaxi.se).

➜ The ridesharing firm Uber (www.uber.com) also covers Stockholm.

Boat

➜ Djurgårdsfärjan city ferry services connect Gröna Lund Tivoli on Djurgården with Nybroplan (summer only) and Slussen (year-round) as frequently as every 10 minutes in summer; SL transport passes and tickets apply.

Tram

➜ The historic 7 tram runs between Norrmalmstorg and Skansen, passing most attractions on Djurgården.

➜ SL transport passes are valid.

Tickets & Passes

➜ **Storstockholms Lokaltrafik** (SL; ☏08-600 10 00; www.sl.se; Centralstationen; ⏱SL Center Sergels Torg 7am-6.30pm Mon-Fri, 10am-5pm Sat & Sun, inside Centralstationen 6.30am-11.45pm Mon-Sat, from 7am Sun) runs the tunnelbana (metro), local trains and buses.

➜ Buy tickets and passes at SL counters, ticket machines at tunnelbana stations, and Pressbyrå kiosks.

➜ The same tickets are valid on the tunnelbana, local trains and buses, and some local ferry routes.

➜ Single tickets are available, but if you're traveling more than once or twice it's better to get a refillable Access card.

➜ A single ticket costs 30kr-60kr and is valid for 75 minutes; it covers return trips and transfers between bus and metro.

➜ A 24-hour/72-hour/seven-day pass costs 120/240/315kr for an adult. Add another 20kr for a refillable Access card.

Essential Information

Business Hours

Except where indicated, we list hours for high season (mid-June to August). Expect more limited hours the rest of the year. Many businesses close early the day before and all day after official public holidays.

➤ **Banks** 9.30am–3pm Monday to Friday; some city branches open to 5pm or 6pm

➤ **Bars & pubs** 11am or noon to 1am or 2am

➤ **Government offices** 9am–5pm Monday to Friday

➤ **Restaurants** 11am–2pm and 5pm–10pm, often closed on Sunday and/or Monday; high-end restaurants often close for a week or two in July or August

➤ **Shops** 9am–6pm Monday to Friday, to 1pm Saturday

Discount Cards

➤ **Stockholm Pass** (🕿 08-663 00 80; www.stockholmpass.com; adult 1-/2-/3-/5-day pass 595/795/995/1295kr, children half-price) is a discount package that includes free sightseeing tours and admission to 75 attractions.

Electricity

Type C
230V/50Hz

Emergency & Important Numbers

➤ 24-hour medical advice 🕿 08-32 0100

➤ Emergency 🕿 112

Money

➤ ATMs are plentiful, but many businesses in Stockholm are now cash-free and accept payment by credit or debit card only.

➤ **Forex-Vasagatan** (Centralplan 15; 🕑 5.30am-10pm Sun-Fri, to 6pm Sat; 🚇 Centralen) money-changers are near the tourist office and Centralstationen.

Public Holidays

Midsummer brings life almost to a halt for three days: transport and other services are reduced, and most shops and smaller tourist offices close, as do some attractions.

Note also that Midsommarafton (Midsummer's Eve), Julafton (Christmas Eve; 24 December) and Nyårsafton (New Year's Eve; 31 December) are not official holidays but are generally nonworking days for most of the population.

Nyårsdag (New Year's Day) 1 January

Trettondag Jul (Epiphany) 6 January

Långfredag, Påsk, Annandag Påsk (Good Friday, Easter Sunday and Monday) March/April

Första Maj (Labour Day) 1 May

Kristi Himmelsfärdsdag (Ascension Day) May/June

Pingst, Annandag

Pingst (Whit Sunday and Monday) Late May or early June

Midsommardag (Midsummer's Day) Saturday between 19 and 25 June

Alla Helgons Dag (All Saints Day) Saturday, late October or early November

Juldag (Christmas Day) 25 December

Annandag Jul (Boxing Day) 26 December

Safe Travel

➡ **Pickpockets** Watch your wallet in crowded, hectic places like Sergels torg and Centralstationen.

➡ **Taxi scams** There's no fee regulation on taxis; check the price list posted in the taxi window and agree on a rate with the driver.

Taxes & Refunds

If you live outside the European Union (EU) you are entitled to a tax refund on your purchases. In Stockholm, Value Added Tax (VAT) is included in the price of items sold. When you buy something at a store displaying a Global Blue Tax-Free Shopping sticker, ask the cashier for a tax-free form. The goods must be in the original package, unused and unopened. Keep your receipts. Then display the form at the Global Blue counter at your last EU airport. This only applies to purchases of more than 200kr.

Telephone

➡ Smartphones are ubiquitous in Stockholm; coin-operated public telephones are virtually nonexistent.

➡ To call abroad from Sweden, dial zero and the country code. Within Sweden, dial the full area code including zero.

Mobile Phones

➡ The main providers are Tre, Telia, Comviq and Telenor.

➡ Buy local SIM cards from Pressbyrå locations, including at Arlanda Airport.

Phone Cards

➡ The few remaining payphones are operated with phonecards purchased from Pressbyrån newsagents (or with a credit card, although this is ludicrously expensive).

➡ Ask for a *telefon kort* for 50kr or 120kr, which roughly equate to 50 minutes and 120 minutes of local talk time, respectively. Be sure to specify you're using the card on a payphone, not refilling a mobile phone.

Money-Saving Tips

➡ Book hotels and domestic travel online in advance. Summer rates are cheaper.

➡ Make lunch your main meal, as the locals do: look for *dagens rätt*, the daily lunch special, usually excellent value even at top-end restaurants (95kr–185kr).

Toilets

Most public toilets charge 5kr or 10kr; pay with 5kr or 10kr coins or via SMS.

Tourist Information

Stockholm Visitor Centre (☑08-50 82 85 08; www.visitstockholm.

Dos & Don'ts

➡ Smoking is banned in all bars, restaurants and hotels.

➡ Take off your shoes inside the front door when visiting a Swedish home.

➡ The most commonly uttered word in Swedish is *tack* – it means 'thanks'. Throw it out there!

com; Kulturhuset, Sergels Torg 3; ◷9am-7pm Mon-Fri, 9am-4pm Sat, 10am-4pm Sun May–mid-Sep, shorter hr rest of year; 🛈; ⓇT-Centralen) The main visitors centre occupies a space inside Kulturhuset on Sergels Torg.

Tourist Centre (✆08-550 882 20; www.guidestock-holm.info; Köpmangatan 22; ◷10am-4pm Mon-Fri year-round, 11am-2pm Sat & Sun Jun-Sep; ⓇGamla Stan) Tiny office in Gamla Stan, with brochures and information.

Visit Djurgården (✆08-667 77 01; www.visitdjurgar-den.se; Djurgårdsvägen 2; ◷9am-dusk) With tourist information specific to Djurgården, this office is at the edge of the Djurgården bridge.

Travellers with Disabilities

➡ Stockholm is one of the easiest cities in which to get around in a wheelchair.

➡ Some street crossings have ramps for wheelchairs and audio signals for visually impaired people, and many grocery stores are wheelchair accessible.

➡ People with disabilities will find transport services, ranging from trains to taxis, with adapted facilities.

➡ Public toilets and some hotel rooms have facilities for those with disabilities.

➡ Download Lonely Planet's free Accessible Travel guide from http://lptravel.to/AccessibleTravel.

Visas

➡ Citizens of EU countries can enter Sweden with a passport or a national identification card (passports are recommended) and stay indefinitely.

➡ Some nationalities will need a Schengen visa, good for 90 days.

➡ Non-EU passport holders from Australia, New Zealand, Canada and the US can enter and stay in Sweden without a visa for up to 90 days.

➡ Citizens of South Africa and many other African, Asian and some eastern European countries require tourist visas for entry to Sweden. These are only available in advance from Swedish embassies (allow two months). Visas are good for any 90 days within a six-month period.

➡ Migrationsverket (www.migrationsverket.se) is the Swedish migration board and handles all applications for visas.

Language

Most Swedish sounds are similar to their English counterparts. One exception is *fh* (a breathy sound pronounced with rounded lips, like saying 'f' and 'w' at the same time), but with a little practice, you'll soon get it right. Note also that *ai* is pronounced as in 'aisle', *aw* as in 'saw', *air* as in 'hair', *eu* as the 'u' in 'nurse', *ew* as the 'ee' in 'see' with rounded lips, and *ey* as the 'e' in 'bet' but longer. Just read our pronunciation guides as if they were English and you'll be understood. The stressed syllables are indicated with italics.

Basics

Hello.
Hej.　　　hey

Goodbye.
Hej då.　　hey daw

Yes.
Ja.　　　yaa

No.
Nej.　　ney

Please.
Tack.　　tak

Thank you (very much).
Tack (så mycket)　　tak (saw *mew*·ke)

You're welcome.
Varsågod.　　var·sha·*gohd*

Excuse me.
Ursäkta mig.　　oor·*shek*·ta mey

Sorry.
Förlåt.　　feur·*lawt*

How are you?
Hur mår du?　　hoor mawr doo

Fine, thanks. And you?
Bra, tack. Och dig?　braa tak o dey

What's your name?
Vad heter du?　　vaad *hey*·ter doo

My name is ...
Jag heter ...　　yaa *hey*·ter ...

Do you speak English?
Talar du engelska?　taa·lar doo eng·el·ska

I don't understand.
Jag förstår inte.　yaa feur·*shtawr in*·te

Eating & Drinking

What would you recommend?
Vad skulle ni rekommendera?
vaad *sku*·le nee re·ko·men·*dey*·ra

Do you have vegetarian food?
Har ni vegetarisk mat?
har nee ve·ge·*taa*·risk maat

I'll have ...
Jag vill ha ...　　yaa vil haa ...

Cheers!
Skål!　　skawl

I'd like (the) ...
Jag skulle vilja ha ...
yaa *sku*·le *vil*·yav haa ...

　bill
　räkningen　　*reyk*·ning·en

　drink list
　drickslistan　　*driks*·lis·tan

　menu
　menyn　　me·*newn*

Emergencies

Help!
Hjälp!　　yelp

Go away!
Försvinn! feur·shvin

Call ...!
Ring ...! ring ...

  a doctor
  efter en doktor ef·ter en dok·tor

  the police
  polisen poh·lee·sen

I'm lost.
Jag har gått vilse. yaa har got vil·se

I'm sick.
Jag är sjuk. yaa air fhook

Where are the toilets?
Var är toaletten? var air toh·aa·le·ten

Transport & Directions

Where's the ...?
Var ligger ...? var li·ger ...

  bank
  banken ban·ken

  post office
  posten pos·ten

  tourist office
  turistinformationen
  too·rist·in·for ma·fhoh·nen

I'd like one ... (to Stockholm) please.
Jag skulle vilja ha en ... (till Stockholm).
yaa sku·le vil·ya haa eyn ... (til stok·holm)

  one-way ticket
  enkelbiljett en·kel·bil·yet

  return ticket
  returbiljett re·toor·bil·yet

What time does the train/bus leave?
När avgår tåget/bussen?
nair aav·gawr taw·get/bu·sen

Can you stop here?
Kan du stanna här?
kan doo sta·na hair

Shopping & Services

I'm looking for ...
Jag letar efter ... yaa ley·tar ef·ter ...

How much is it?
Hur mycket kostar det?
hoor mew·ke kos·tar de

Time & Numbers

What time is it?
Hur mycket är klockan?
hur mew·ke air klo·kan

It's (two) o'clock.
Klockan är (två). klo·kan air (tvaw)

in the morning
på förmiddagen paw feur·mi·daa·gen

in the afternoon
på eftermiddagen paw ef·ter·mi·daa·gen

yesterday
igår ee·gawr

tomorrow
imorgon ee·mor·ron

1	*ett*	et
2	*två*	tvaw
3	*tre*	trey
4	*fyra*	few·ra
5	*fem*	fem
6	*sex*	seks
7	*sju*	fhoo
8	*åtta*	o·ta
9	*nio*	nee·oh
10	*tio*	tee·oh
100	*ett hundra*	et hun·dra
1000	*ett tusen*	et too·sen

Behind the Scenes

Send Us Your Feedback

We love to hear from travellers – your comments help make our books better. We read every word, and we guarantee that your feedback goes straight to the authors. Visit **lonelyplanet.com/contact** to submit your updates and suggestions.

Note: We may edit, reproduce and incorporate your comments in Lonely Planet products such as guidebooks, websites and digital products, so let us know if you don't want your comments reproduced or your name acknowledged. For a copy of our privacy policy visit lonelyplanet.com/privacy.

Our Readers

Many thanks to the travellers who used the last edition and wrote to us with helpful hints, useful advice and interesting anecdotes:

Annah Grubb, Axel Nelms, Camilla Jensen, Charles Lunberg, Georgia Fenwick, Laure Marcellesi, Maria Casadei, Mikael Vesterberg, Steen Bach-Vilhelmsen

Acknowledgements

Cover photograph: Gamla Stan, Luigi Vaccarella/4Corners ©

Contents photograph (p4–5): Södermalm, Cranjam/Getty ©

Becky's Thanks

Thanks to my mom, Christina, for rounding up a bunch of extra info from her friends; Paul Smith for inspiring the pinball quest; James Borup for the brewery intel; the Auld Dub in general; and all the various editors in-house at Lonely Planet for helping whip the resulting content into shape.

This Book

This 4th edition of Lonely Planet's *Pocket Stockholm* guidebook was researched and written by Becky Ohlsen and curated by Charles Rawlings-Way. The previous edition was also written by Becky Ohlsen. This guidebook was produced by the following:

Destination Editor Gemma Graham

Product Editors Ronan Abayawickrema, Paul Harding

Senior Cartographers David Kemp, Valentina Kremenchutskaya

Book Designer Gwen Cotter

Assisting Editors Janet Austin, Chris Pitts

Cover Researcher Naomi Parker

Thanks to Sandie Kestell, Genna Patterson, Rachel Rawling, Jessica Ryan, Gabrielle Stefanos, Angela Tinson, Tony Wheeler

Index

See also separate subindexes for:

⊗ **Eating p157**

⊖ **Drinking p158**

☆ **Entertainment p158**

🄰 **Shopping p158**

⊗ Eating

SORINA CHIRITA

LONELY PLANET IN THE WILD

Our Writers

Charles Rawlings-Way

Charles is a veteran travel writer who has penned 30-something titles for Lonely Planet – including guides to Singapore, Toronto, Sydney, Tasmania, New Zealand, the South Pacific and Australia – and numerous articles. After dabbling in the dark arts of architecture, cartography and project management, and busking for some years, Charles hit the road for LP in 2005, and hasn't stopped travelling since.

Becky Ohlsen

Becky is a freelance writer, editor and critic based in Portland, Oregon. She writes guidebooks and travel stories about Scandinavia, Portland and elsewhere for Lonely Planet. Though raised in the mountains of Colorado, Becky has been exploring Sweden since childhood, while visiting her grandparents and other relatives in Stockholm and parts north. She's thoroughly hooked on pickled herring and saffron ice cream but has nothing good to say about Swedish beer.

Published by Lonely Planet Global Limited
CRN 554153
4th edition – April 2018
ISBN 978 1 78657 456 5
© Lonely Planet 2018 Photographs © as indicated 2018
10 9 8 7 6 5 4 3 2 1
Printed in China

31192021477649